THE ZULU KINGS
AND
THEIR ARMIES

THE ZULU KINGS

AND

THEIR ARMIES

by

Jonathan Sutherland

and

Diane Canwell

Pen & Sword
MILITARY

First published in Great Britain in 2004 by
Pen & Sword Military
an imprint of
Pen & Sword Books Ltd
47 Church Street
Barnsley
South Yorkshire
S70 2AS

ISBN 1 84415 060 7

A CIP catalogue record for this book is
available from the British Library

Typeset in 11/13 Sabon by
Phoenix Typesetting, Auldgirth, Dumfriesshire

Printed and bound in England by
CPI UK

Pen & Sword Books Ltd incorporates the imprints of Pen & Sword
Aviation, Pen & Sword Maritime, Pen & Sword Military, Wharncliffe
Local History, Pen & Sword Select, Pen & Sword Military Classics
and Leo Cooper.

For a complete list of Pen & Sword titles please contact
PEN & SWORD BOOKS LIMITED
47 Church Street, Barnsley, South Yorkshire, S70 2AS, England
E-mail: enquiries@pen-and-sword.co.uk
Website: www.pen-and-sword.co.uk

Contents

Dedicated to the Revd Kenneth Smith MBE MA

Glossary of Zulu Military Terms

Single	Plural	Description
isAngoma	izAngoma	A Zulu diviner or witchdoctor
iBandla	amaBandla	The members of a tribal council or a tribal assembly
iBandla imhlope	amaBandla imhlope	A married Zulu regiment required to muster at the orders of the king
iBeshu	amaBeshu	A calfskin flap used to cover the buttocks
umBumbulozo	–	A smaller form of war shield used from the 1850s
iButho	amaButho	A regiment of Zulu warriors based on their age groups
isiCoco	iziCoco	A married warrior's head ring made from fibres coated in gum and charcoal and polished with beeswax
uDibi	izinDibi	A teenage Zulu who accompanied the Zulu army as a mat carrier, but not yet old enough to join a regiment
inDuna	izinDuna	A Zulu state official appointed by either the Zulu king or a chieftain. Usually an advisor, but in military terms, a commander of a group of warriors
isiFuba	iziFuba	The chest or centre of a traditional Zulu battle formation
isiGaba	iziGaba	A group of related amaViyo in an iButho

Single	Plural	Description
isiGodlo	iziGodlo	The king's living area in a kraal, or an area in the kraal used by the royal family, particularly his women
iGwalagwala	–	The tail feathers of a lourie bird, usually greenish-black or purple, used by high ranking warriors in their headdress
inGxotha	izinGxotha	A brass armband given to warriors by the king for bravery
isiHlangu	iziHlangu	A large regimental war shield
isiJula	iziJula	A short-bladed throwing spear
iKhanda	amaKhanda	A military kraal established by the king to house a regiment
iKhehla	amaKhehla	A married Zulu warrior who is allowed to wear a head ring
uKhonto	imiKhonto	A general name for a spear
umKhosi	imiKhosi	The annual ceremony held prior to a harvest
umKhumbi	imiKhumbi	An assembly of warriors, usually in a circle
isiKhulu	iziKhulu	A high ranking warrior, a member of the Zulu hierarchy, or a member of the council of elders, literally meaning 'great one'
inKosi	amaKosi	A king or chieftain
uKukleza	–	The drinking of milk symbolically and actually from the udders of a cow, indicating that a young Zulu warrior has enlisted in a regiment
iKlwa	amaKlwa	Zulu name for the stabbing spear, or assegai
iLobolo	–	Cattle paid as a dowry by the groom and his family to the family of the bride
isiLomo	iziLomo	A brave warrior who has become a favourite of the king
iMpi	iziImpi	Meaning war, but used as a name to describe the Zulu army
iNcequ	iziNcequ	A servant or attendant of a chief or the king

Single	Plural	Description
iNdwa	–	The feathers of a blue crane used in the headdresses of high ranking warriors
isiNene	iziNene	Twisted furs usually from a monkey or a civet used to hang from the front on a waistband
iNkatha	iziNkatha	The sacred grass coil of the Zulu nation
umNcedo	abaNcedo	A plaited sheath to cover a man's genitals
iNsizwa	iziNsizwa	An unmarried young man
iNtwana	abaNtwana	A prince, usually the son of the king and hence a member of the royal family
umNumzane	abaNumzane	The head of a Zulu household
umNyanga	iziNyanga	A Zulu herbal doctor
isiPhapha	iziPhapha	A Zulu throwing spear with a short and broad blade, usually used for hunting
uPhaphe	oPhaphe	Feathers used to decorate a headdress
iPhovela	amaPhovela	Headdresses made of cow skin, usually worn by unmarried regiments, with the appearance of two horns
uPondo	izimPondo	The horns, wings or flanks (left and right) in the traditional Zulu battle formation
umQhele	imiQhele	A warrior's headband made from fur filled with bulrushes or cow dung. Senior regiments would use otter skin and junior regiments, leopard skin. Warriors would also have amaBheqe (ear flaps) made from monkey skin
isiQu	iziQu	A Zulu bravery necklace made from interlocking beads or sections of willow, presented to warriors by the king
iSakabuli	–	Tail feathers from a longtailed widow, fixed to a headband by porcupine quills and worn on a warrior's headdress
iShoba	amaShoba	Tufted cow tails used as arm and leg decorations (sometimes necklaces)
amaSi	–	Curdled milk

Single	Plural	Description
umShokobezi	imiShokobezi	Another description of cow tail decorations worn on the arms and legs
inTanga	–	A group of Zulu men or women born within four or five years of one another who have been formed into a group
inTelezi	izinTelezi	Protective medicines and potions sprinkled on warriors prior to going into battle
umThakathi	abaThakathi	A wizard or sorcerer
umuThi	imiThi	Herbal medicines believed to have protective properties or supernatural powers
umuTsha	imiTsha	A Zulu loin cloth consisting of a cow hide belt with a flap over the buttocks and twisted animal fur hanging from the front
uTshwala	–	A sorghum beer, high in nutrients
umuVa	imiVa	The reserve or loins of a Zulu army
iViyo	amaViyo	A company of Zulu warriors, variably between 50 and 150
iWisa	amaWisa	A knobkerrie or war club
inYanga	izinYanga	A Zulu herbalist
umuZi	imiZi	A family kraal also describing the civilians living in that kraal

Introduction

The powerful Zulu nation was created in the early nineteenth century by Shaka kaSenzangakhona, but in little more than sixty years it would be utterly crushed by the British.

Under the rules of Shaka, Dingane, Mpande, Cetshwayo and Dinuzulu the Zulu spread terror throughout Southern Africa, sparking wars, mass migrations and slaughter. Yet the Zulu were no savages; they were a highly complex society with a united identity. Above all they were an effective and efficient military machine, capable of outwitting experienced professional European troops and their over-confident commanders.

For many the Zulu are personified by the two feature films *Zulu* (1964) and *Zulu Dawn* (1979) which provide highly fictionalized accounts of Rorke's Drift and Isandlwana. The first a little more than a footnote in the history of the Anglo-Zulu War of 1879 and the latter a crushing defeat inflicted on the British by the Zulu when they slaughtered an over-confident invasion column.

The Zulu remain a dominant and numerous force in Southern Africa. Approximately eight million speak Zulu in South Africa, six million of which are concentrated in the province of KwaZulu-Natal. Collectively the Zulu account for twenty per cent of the South African population. Their culture, language and identity is clearly felt throughout the country.

Less than 200 years ago the Zulu were an insignificant Nguni tribe, but in the early nineteenth century Shaka's conquests forged an efficient fighting force from his tiny tribe. He revolutionized

1

warfare in the region and began to create an empire. As an independent entity his conquests would last barely sixty years.

Arguably, Shaka invented the assegai, a short, stabbing spear, not unlike a Roman gladius, designed specifically for close-quarters fighting. In the pre-Shaka period, warfare was restricted to lines of men throwing spears at one another until one side broke and fled. Modest reparations were extracted, tributes and hostages taken. The former warring tribes would then be content to live alongside one another until a new reason developed for conflict. Shaka revolutionized this too; a defeated tribe would be absorbed into his new empire, their cultural identity submerged and replaced with the Zulu way of life.

Shaka's battlefield tactics relied on rapid movement, based on the army's ability to outmanoeuvre the enemy. Shaka adopted a form familiar to the Zulu; the bull's head and horns-shaped semi-circle. At the heart of the army was the bull's head, a formation of troops who would advance straight onto the enemy, pinning his main force and demanding his attention. Meanwhile the Zulu wings, or bull's horns, would fan out left and right with the intention of encircling the enemy force. The Zulu reserves, or the loins, were positioned to the rear to be unleashed or deployed when needed. Such was the battle lust of the Zulu that the loins were often required to face away from the battlefield in order to keep them calm.

Once the battle was underway the Zulu army would continue to attack until the enemy was completely crushed. Little quarter was given or expected. In this way an enemy army, utterly defeated and bereft of its leaders, could be more easily absorbed into the empire.

In the early years the Zulu army, armed with assegais and large cowhide shields, carried all before it. When firearms entered the region the Zulu were never proficient at using these weapons, favouring the opportunity to engage in close combat with the enemy in order to prove their bravery.

Shaka's reign was short and he was succeeded by his half-brother, Dingane. From the beginning of Dingane's rule the inevitable collision with white settlers, notably in the form of the Boer and later the British, would spell the end of Zulu dominance in Southern Africa. A disastrous defeat at the hands of the Boer at the Battle of Blood River on the Ncome River in 1838 sufficiently undermined Dingane, to allow his half-brother, Mpande, to succeed in 1840. The influence of the British was increasing in the region and this would culminate in Sir Bartle Frere, the British High Commissioner, delivering an ultimatum to Cetshwayo, who now ruled the Zulu, to disband his army.

The reforms demanded by the British would not only undermine the Zulus' ability to protect themselves, but also radically affect the entire Zulu way of life. War became inevitable and five British columns entered Zululand in 1879 with the purpose of converging on Cetshwayo's capital, oNdini (Ulundi). The British were soundly beaten and outmanoeuvred at Isandlwana (22 January 1879). On the same day several Zulu regiments, against the express orders of Cetshwayo, crossed into Natal and attacked Rorke's Drift. It was held by Company B, 2/24th, and a number of auxiliaries. The tiny garrison held out for over ten hours and the British awarded eleven Victoria Crosses and showered other honours on the defenders. It could not, however, wipe out the stinging defeat at Isandlwana which had claimed the lives of over 1,300 men.

For a time the invasion was stalled and in March the Zulu scored another victory at the battle of Hlobane (28 March 1879). Lord Chelmsford, in overall command of the British forces, knew that his career and reputation was teetering on the brink of disaster. Already the British government had dispatched Sir Garnet Wolseley to succeed Chelmsford. But just short of Cetshwayo's capital on 4 July 1879 a formidable British square shattered the Zulus' last hope of denying the British.

In time Cetshwayo, who had fled the scene, was captured and exiled. It would be several years before he would be allowed to return to his kingdom and his people. By then the kingdom had been partitioned and Cetshwayo would be forced to fight to regain his throne. Cetshwayo was decisively defeated at the second battle of oNdini on 21 July 1883 and on 8 February 1884, probably as a result of poisoning, the last independent king of the Zulu was dead.

Cetshwayo's successor, Dinuzulu, ultimately had to rely on the

Boers to install him as the new king. In return the Boers were rewarded by vast farms which only sought to undermine Dinuzulu's position. This prompted the British to annexe Zululand in May 1887. Dinuzulu would find himself in exile until 1898, but the ill-feeling between the different Zulu factions smouldered, culminating in a Zulu uprising in 1906. It was ruthlessly crushed at the Battle of Mome Gorge (10 June 1906). Dinuzulu was hopelessly implicated and was found guilty of rebellion. He was not released until South Africa gained its own independence in 1910, but he would survive just three more years.

The coverage of this book spans nearly 100 years from the pre-Shaka period, through the rules of the Zulu kings, until the final demise of Dinuzulu. At its height, the Zulu army could muster 40,000, perhaps as many as 50,000 troops, yet these were no regular soldiers. They were part time soldiery who were required to serve from the age of eighteen. It is the Zulu army system which moulded the Zulu nation. Warriors were assigned to regiments according to their age rather than their tribal affiliations. It is therefore unsurprising that when the British delivered the ultimatum to Cetshwayo in December 1878 to disband the Zulu regimental system, the Zulu feared that their entire way of life was under threat.

Ultimately the Zulu would realize that the raw courage which had brought them through the conflicts and battles up to Isandlwana would no longer ensure victory. British weapons would now prove too powerful for them but the spirit of the army would not be finally extinguished until 1906.

Chapter One

Bantu Warfare

It is not clear exactly where the Bantu, or as correctly written, the Aba'Ntu (meaning people, the plural of UmuNtu or man) originally derived. It seems that around 10,000 years ago they passed along the Nile Valley and into what is now known as the Sudan. They existed as nomadic herders and would have the bulk of the sparsely populated African continent almost to themselves. Ultimately they would encounter the Bushmen and the Hottentots, who had passed along the same route some time before them.

The Aba'Ntu entered East Africa then Central Africa, always heading south to better weather and grazing for their herds. Progress, passage and direction was always impeded and influenced by natural barriers, such as rivers and mountain ranges. Indeed by the fourteenth century their way was dictated by the Kalahari Dessert. Here they expanded to the west, forcing the Hottentots against the Atlantic Ocean. They then proceeded down the coast.

At some point they changed direction to the south-east and by the sixteenth century were established in what is now known as the Transvaal. This group of Aba'Ntu were the Nguni with a common language, but soon intermarriage with other clans, such as the Venda-Karanga splintered the groups. Pure Nguni moved into the area between the Drakensberg Mountains and the Indian Ocean, easily pushing aside the scattered Bushmen in the region. Here they stopped in the fertile river valleys. At this time three of the Nguni clan groups settled in the Natal region (Mtetwa, Lala and the Debe). The Tonga headed north and the Xhosa and the Ntungwa spread into the south.

In 1652 the Europeans arrived on the Cape, but the nearest Aba'Ntu was still over 800 kilometres to the north. Indeed the Dutch, who had established this first European settlement, and the Aba'Ntu were not destined to meet for another 120 years.

In the Natal region there were at least 800 different clans. Some were very small, but others reached strengths of around 10,000. Even at this early stage practices which would be more overtly used by Shaka and his successors became commonplace. Chieftains would often murder their potential successors in order to cement their own position. Whilst strong clans lived alongside weaker tribes around them, many of the weaker clans became absorbed. A chieftain would not countenance allowing a neighbouring tribe to gain in strength for fear that his own position would be challenged. Inter-tribal marriages were commonplace in order to prevent possible inbreeding. Not all marriages were by mutual clan consent. Wives would be taken as tribute and in some cases the women of the bushmen were also taken in the frequent raids that took place.

By the middle of the eighteenth century the region was dominated by the Sutu-Nguni. The coastal strip had become overpopulated but now, with the arrival of the Europeans, the traditional nomadic existence of the Aba'Ntu was no longer possible. It was in this area, for better or worse, the seeds of the Zulu people were scattered.

As herders, the Aba'Ntu's existence was driven by the needs of their cattle. The possession of these long-horned cattle was the basis upon which a chieftain could compare his wealth. The clans would also keep goats and sheep; these would be used as a form of currency of lower denominations than cattle. It was the herd which bound the clans together; a chieftain with a royal herd would disperse his cattle amongst the various kraals (settlements) in order to ensure that they had sufficient grazing. Kraals would also allow their cattle to be maintained by other kraals, with the two settlements sharing any increases in the herd. Cattle were also used in taxation, loans, fines and, above all, the purchase price or lobola for a wife. Purchase is, perhaps, misleading, since a wife was only ever exchanged for cattle. If the wife was returned to her parents, the lobola was refunded. Wives who could not produce offspring for their husband were often replaced with their sister. Women, therefore, were valuable as an economic resource as cattle and a woman's status was determined by the lobola placed upon her.

The Aba'Ntu were polygamous. A normal man could have as many as three or four wives; petty chieftains could have twenty, whilst significant chieftains may have had several hundred wives. A chieftain would select one of his wives as a Great Wife, for which he would have paid a significant lobola. A Great Wife did not tend to be the first wife which he had purchased. His wealth early in his married life would preclude the purchase of an expensive Great Wife. The offspring of the Great Wife would become the chieftain's only recognized successors.

The importance of cattle went deeper as milk curds (amaSi) were the staple diet. In any kraal the cattle pen would be located at the centre and the herd would be milked at noon and always returned to the pen at night. Beneath the kraal, in clay-lined pits, the clan would store its winter grain. The people lived in hive-shaped, grass-thatched structures made from woven saplings. Each hut had a single, low entrance and within the smoky interior earthenware pots would be used for cooking on an open fire. The positioning of each of the huts was according to the status of the woman of the hut. A Great Wife's hut was usually positioned at the far side of the gate into the settlement. Next to her would be the first wife's hut and then less important wives after that. The huts housing unmarried warriors were set aside from the women's huts and the sons and daughters, along with other retainers, would have their huts positioned nearest the gate. The whole settlement was surrounded by a pen with thorns in order to provide a deterrent to wild animals and possible attackers. Inside each hut the floor was covered with polished clay and cow dung. Whilst the huts were alive with vermin, they could be pulled down and replaced in a matter of a few days. The huts were rainproof, providing warmth in the winter months and relative cool in the summer.

The size of each of the kraals largely depended upon the number of wives a man possessed. Important chieftains may have had to house several dozen wives and a few thousand warriors. Children were born into a complex society. It was unusual for a child to even see their own father until they had been fully weaned. Indeed, their father would not share their mother's hut until this time. All of their father's other wives were considered to be mothers and if their father had brothers, these would be fathers. If a mother produced twins or triplets then all but one of the children would be suffocated and if a child was born with a defect it too would have a clod of earth stuffed into its mouth.

The Zulu were obsessed with hygiene and the possibility of contamination. Male children in particular were subjected to strengthening ceremonies, such as being buried to the neck in a hole. For at least the first five years, a child would have the almost exclusive attention of its mother, but at this age would then be expected to help look after younger children. A male child, by the time he was six or seven, could well have been expected to help look after the sheep and goats. Progressively, as the child got older, he would be given the ultimate responsibility of helping to look after the cattle herd. He would be expected to fight for grazing with the young boys of neighbouring kraals. When the boy entered puberty he was expected to take the kraal's cattle out and hide from the rest of the kraal. It was considered auspicious if the kraal and its warriors took a considerable time to find him and the cattle. A feast would follow and he would be given his first assegai.

The boy would be part of a group of children his own age and a leader amongst the boys would be chosen. This group was known as an iNtanga. In effect this was the beginning of a regiment. Clearly, dependent upon the size of the clan, a small iNtanga could consist of only several boys, but in larger kraals several dozen would form an iNtanga. As the boys reached the age of eighteen they would be officially drafted or enrolled into a regiment in a ceremony known as ukuButhwa. Prior to that, if the boys were required in war, they would operate as food or beer carriers and would care for the cattle which would be slaughtered en route to feed the warriors. They would also be expected to carry mats or additional shields for the more senior warriors. These boys, usually aged between twelve and fifteen years, were collectively known as izindibi. Singularly they were known as udibi. The purpose of this was to make the boys even hardier than before, as they would have to carry and protect relatively heavy loads and always keep up with the warriors. This would also give the boys an opportunity to see a little more of the world. By the time the boy came of age he would be considered old enough to become a warrior and he had fought other boys with sticks, hunted small animals, dealt with the dangers of protecting goats, sheep and cattle and had accompanied warriors into campaigns. Once the ukuButhwa had been carried out the boys were now considered adults and warriors. Their lives would change and for many months of the year they would be expected to carry out services for the chieftain, such as looking after his cattle, in return for which he would support them.

The iNtangas were ultimately controlled by an inDuna, who was answerable directly to the clan chieftain. An inDuna was not only an administrator in as much as he dealt with disputes and collected taxes, but he also had military responsibilities. He would become the leader of the iNtangas in his region in times of war. iNtanga leaders appointed by the inDuna would hold that position for life. The iNtanga would continue to recruit members from a particular neighbourhood until it was considered that they had enough members to form a regiment. Once this figure had been reached the iNtanga would no longer recruit.

Religion and witchcraft played an important role in the kraal's existence. Elaborate ceremonies took place to strengthen the army and the chieftain before war, during which a bull would be strangled by the bare hands of warriors. After battle a more elaborate ceremony was involved if a warrior had killed one of the enemies. The aba'Ntu believed that a warrior who had killed an enemy was in grave danger of madness. Routinely a warrior would slash open the abdomen of the fallen enemy to allow his spirit to escape. For a time, before he was cleansed, he would sleep separately from the other warriors and if he had intercourse with his wife it was believed he would pass the disease on to her. In these early times, therefore, military campaigns were brief as the cleansing rituals required the men to deal with the situation as soon as possible for fear of developing the madness.

Conflicts tended to arise from the most superficial of reasons, such as a low lobola being offered for a bride, or a supposed slight or lack of respect. Outright aggressiveness was rare, but the primary cause for any conflict tended to be encroachment. The purpose of any warfare was to drive an encroaching clan, or a weaker neighbour, away to ensure that the clan retained the grazing rights to a particular area. Up to twenty-five per cent of the male population of a clan would be mustered by iNtanga. The iNtangas would operate together as an impi, which was a generic term used for any type of military force, regardless of size. The vast majority of battles, or skirmishes, were decided by sheer weight of numbers. In effect, warfare was simply an extension of hunting. The vast majority of aba'Ntu would approach the enemy to within around 60 metres and hurl a 2 metre spear. This preliminary bombardment could well settle the issue; if not, further spears would be thrown. If it appeared that there would have to be hand-to-hand fighting, some warriors would retain one of their spears for stabbing, whilst others chose to use a knobkerrie, which was a stick with a heavy end used for bashing.

For defensive purposes the aba'Ntu used an oval, cowhide shield approximately 1 metre across. It was well braced and capable of deflecting a thrown spear. It would also be used offensively in a mêleé to batter the opponent off balance, allowing the warrior to stab with his spear, or bring his knobkerrie down on the man's head.

The vast majority of conflicts were, in fact, pre-arranged battles. In many cases the impis would be accompanied by their women and children, who would watch the conflict from the relative safety of a nearby hill. They would provide spectator support for their own warriors. Before any spears were thrown, the braver or more arrogant warriors from either side would taunt the enemy (giya). Once this had taken place, the two impis would move closer to one another, throwing spears until in the majority of cases one side broke and fled. It was comparatively rare that the two impis would even close to combat. The losing impi would have to pay a ransom for any captives, usually in cattle, and would obviously lose some land. The victor would not seek to eliminate the opposing clan.

10

A numerical advantage was the only tactic usually adopted and in these cases a battle rarely took place; the smaller clan would simply capitulate. If a clan was effectively forced out of its territory and its kraals were now occupied by a larger clan, it would simply move on and find a smaller clan to displace. Ultimately tiny clans would disappear. There were few cases when an entire clan was slaughtered, but without a kraal and lacking cattle they would be forced into the bush and would have to rely on marauding as their sole means of sustenance. If an enemy clan or marauders appeared near a kraal, the cattle would be immediately driven out in order to reduce the value of attacking the kraal. It would then take the marauders some time to locate the cattle and would, in more cases than not, simply move on. Any damage caused to the kraals could be easily repaired and a new kraal could be built in a matter of days.

It was into this society and modes of war that Shaka was born. His father, Senzangakhona, was a young, petty chieftain of the Zulu. Shaka would transform the unsophisticated warfare of the Nguni. It was now 1787.

Chapter Two

Shaka kaSenzangakhona

Shaka was probably born in 1787, at a time when Napoleon Bonaparte was a military student in France. It is this accident of coincidence which has led many to describe Shaka as the African Napoleon. Their lives could not have been more different, however.

Shaka's father, Senzangakhona, was born around the time when the Nguni was ruled by a chieftain called Jobe (chieftain of the Mtetwa), an old man who was due to be succeeded by Tana. Tana had a younger brother called Godongwana and together the two plotted to hasten Jobe's departure. Their plot was discovered and Jobe sent an impi to raid Tana's kraal. Tana was killed and his wounded brother fled. At some point Godongwana changed his name to Dingiswayo (the troubled one). Dingiswayo would become hugely influential in Shaka's life.

After a short time Dingiswayo returned to his homeland to discover that the throne was now held by a younger brother, Mawewe. It was immediately obvious to all concerned that the stranger, who had returned on a horse and armed with a gun, was none other than Godongwana. Interestingly, Dingiswayo had probably met a white man by the name of Robert Cowan, who he had served as a guide. Cowan died, possibly from a fever, and Dingiswayo took his horse and gun. Mawewe fled, but to secure his succession Dingiswayo managed to lure him back and have him murdered.

Dingiswayo inherited a Mtetwa army of little more than 500

men, yet he was determined to increase the influence of his clan. He began by absorbing weaker clans around him and, of course, incorporating their men into his army. In his eight years of reign Dingiswayo managed to absorb at least fifty large clans and many dozens of smaller ones. Over the years Dingiswayo also succeeded in halting the intertribal conflicts in his region.

To the north-west of Dingiswayo's Mtetwa was a small and rather insignificant clan known as the Zulu. They were ruled by Senzangakhona and the 1,500 or so Zulu held a handful of kraals in the Umfolozi Valley. Their immediate neighbours were the eLangeni and indeed Senzangakhona's mother was an eLangeni by birth. The eLangeni's chieftain had recently died and one of his orphans was a girl named Nandi. She and Senzangakhona met secretly and the result found Nandi pregnant. In local terms this was a scandal and Senzangakhona denied the responsibility for Nandi's pregnancy, claiming that she merely had an intestinal beetle (an iShaka) which had caused the swelling of her stomach. Nonetheless Nandi did give birth and reluctantly Senzangakhona made her his third wife and they named their son Shaka. Both the Zulu and the eLangeni were scandalized by the birth and the relationship, and although the couple later produced a daughter, Nomcoba, the relationship was always a stormy one. In order to keep Nandi and her children in the background, Senzangakhona moved her and the children around the different Zulu kraals. Senzangakhona's first wife, Mkabi, hated Nandi. The Zulu elders ignored her and the children and the other Zulu treated them all with contempt. Around the time when Shaka reached the age of six years old he had taken up his duties as a herder. The story is confused, but apparently a dog killed one of Senzangakhona's goats or sheep which Shaka had supposed to have been guarding. Senzangakhona was livid and he banished Nandi, Shaka and Nomcoba back to the eLangeni. The situation could not have been worse; not only had Nandi disgraced the eLangeni by falling pregnant out of marriage, but they now had to return the lobola to the Zulu. For the next ten years or so Shaka became a herd boy for the eLangeni. He was continually bullied and taunted. Without a father and an ostracized mother he became a brooding, ruthless and vengeful young man.

In 1802 a famine struck the area and Nandi had no husband or cattle and the eLangeni evicted her and the children from their kraals. She lived for a time with Gendeyana with whom she bore a son, Njwadi. Nandi was still married technically to Senzangakhona and this was outright adultery. By now Shaka was a tall and impressive young man and both the eLangeni and the Zulu wanted him back. Shaka had only seen his father once in the intervening years, at the time when he had officially reached puberty. They had argued and Shaka had refused to accept his father's offering of his first loin skin (umuTsha). Nandi and the children ignored both the eLangeni and the Zulu and moved instead to live with an aunt who was a member of the emDletsheni, who were part of Jobe's Mtetwa.

For the next six years, firstly under Jobe and then Dingiswayo, Shaka developed into full manhood. He was already showing strong leadership ability. He lived with his mother and sister, with their new foster father, Mbiya. When Shaka was twenty-three Dingiswayo called up the emDletsheni intanga and Shaka became a member of the iziCwe; he was now an Mtetwa warrior.

The iziCwe played a full part in Dingiswayo's continuing policy of expansion. Shaka's policy from the outset was entirely different from that of Dingiswayo. Whilst the monarch favoured political absorption, Shaka favoured a complete crushing of a clan in order to ensure that they never rose up against their conquerors in the future. Shaka felt that shows of military might were far less effective in the longer term than a bloody and total victory on the battlefield.

Shaka is credited with being influential in changing the traditional Bantu tactics of going into battle armed with a throwing spear. He reasoned that having thrown the spear, unless armed with additional spears, warriors were defenceless. He is credited with having created the stabbing assegai which became known as the iKlwa, so called because the name is onomatopoeic for the sound the blade makes when it is pulled out of a body. Shaka advocated using the shield as an offensive weapon; rather than simply defending against thrown spears, warriors would now run into contact with the enemy. Using their shield they would hook the opponent's shield and either spin them off balance or at least expose their chest area for a thrust with the iKlwa. Shaka also advocated dispensing with ox-hide sandals, preferring his warriors to run barefoot to increase their speed potential and balance.

Shaka was able to demonstrate his tactics when the iziCwe were deployed against Pungashe, the Buthelezi chieftain. Interestingly, amongst the ranks of the Buthelezi was one of Shaka's own half-brothers, Bakuza. Shaka and his regiment advanced to within 100 metres of the enemy. In typical Bantu style a Buthelezi warrior came forward to taunt the Mtetwa. Shaka sprang forward to attack the Buthelezi warrior. The enemy threw his spear but it glanced off Shaka's shield. He dealt with a second thrown spear and then hooked his shield behind the enemy and spitted the Buthelezi with his iKlwa. Not content with that, Shaka then charged the whole Buthelezi army alone. He was quickly followed by the rest of his regiment; the Buthelezi fled and in the pursuit Bakuza was killed and Pungashe's Buthelezi were forced to surrender to Dingiswayo. This action by Shaka brought him to Dingiswayo's attention. Indeed the two men had much in common; they had both been disinherited by their fathers.

The victory over the Buthelezi had also brought the Zulu into the sphere of influence of the Mtetwa. Bakuza had been Senzangakhona's preferred heir, but Senzangakhona was summoned by Dingiswayo and told that Shaka was his preferred successor when the time came. At the meeting Senzangakhona agreed, but instead named Sigujana as his heir.

Meanwhile, Shaka was given command of the iziCwe regiment and he set about forming what would become the blueprint for his Zulu army in the future. Again arguably, Shaka is credited with having created the famed bull's head formation. It is said that he divided his regiment into three sections; the largest was the chest which would face the enemy head-on. Two other groups were formed to create the horns which would, in battle, seek to envelop the enemy. The chest was also supported by a reserve which would become known as the loins. These men would replace wounded or exhausted warriors in the front line. Shaka also recruited older herd boys aged around fifteen. One of these boys, known as uDibi, was assigned to every three warriors. They would not only carry the men's sleeping mats but also their food and additional assegais.

In 1816 Senzangakhona died and Dingiswayo, labouring under the misapprehension that Shaka's father still intended that Shaka should be his heir, released him temporarily from his service to press his claim. Shaka sent his half-brother, Ngwadi, ahead to warn the Zulu he was coming. Somehow, by the time Shaka arrived, Sigujana was already dead; he may have been drowned by Ngwadi in a nearby river. Although out of the scope of this military history, Shaka then proceeded to impale any Zulu or eLangeni who had, at any time, humiliated or slighted him or his mother.

Shaka now set about creating the nucleus of the Zulu army which could not have exceeded more than around 400 men. Nonetheless he created four regiments. Mature, male Zulu had previously been allowed to sew a isiCoco (fibre ring) into their hair to show that they were ready for marriage. Shaka made all, but those who had previous military experience, remove their isiCoco. The married, older men became the amaWombe (the battlers) and the remaining mature men became the uJubingqwana and the umGamule, which he usually brigaded together as the izimPohlo (bachelor's brigade). The remaining young bachelors became the uFasimba (the haze); these would become Shaka's favourite regiment and indeed a prototype for all his future regiments.

Dingiswayo clearly hoped that Shaka would create a buffer kingdom, but Shaka would have to tread carefully, as if it ever appeared to Dingiswayo that he would be in a position to challenge him, the monarch would crush the Zulu without question. The first clan to feel the growing power of the Zulu was the eLangeni. Shaka's army surrounded their principle kraal shortly after dawn one morning. Having identified any individual who had slighted him or his mother, they were then taken away and impaled. The rest of the clan, principally the men, effectively became Zulu.

Over the next short period of time Shaka continued to absorb smaller clans. His next major objective was Pungashe's Buthelezi. Pungashe had been defeated by Dingiswayo in the past, but he did not fear the Zulu. Pungashe's army numbered around 600, whilst Shaka could muster something around 750 men. The exact site of the battle between Pungashe and Shaka is unclear, but what little is known is that the uFasimba took up the centre position, supported by the Belebele, whilst half of the izimPohlo formed the right horn and the other half the left. Shaka's army advanced in dense columns so as to disguise their strength. At around 100 metres from the Buthelezi, Shaka ordered the regiments to deploy and show their shields; it was only then that Pungashe realized that he was outnumbered. The uFasimba advanced first with Shaka positioned just behind them, leading the Belebele. At sixty metres they charged and slammed into the Buthelezi ranks. Simultaneously, the Zulu horns closed around the Buthelezi, slaughtering non-combatants who had come to watch the Zulu being defeated.

The battle was short and bloody; Pungashe fled and would ultimately seek refuge with Zwide, the chieftain of the Ndwandwe (Zwide learned what he could from Pungashe and later had him assassinated). The Zulu slaughtered all of the old Buthelezi and burned their kraals. Those who survived were incorporated into the Zulu tribe. As an act of subservience to Dingiswayo, Shaka sent the captured Buthelezi cattle as a gift to his king, but Dingiswayo returned the majority of them.

By the spring of 1817 Shaka had quadrupled his territory. He could now call upon 2,000 warriors, the largest regiment numbering 800 with the uFasimba. Despite having blooded themselves in battle, none of his junior regiments were allowed to marry.

Around this time Shaka received news that his foster father, Mbiya, was dying and, at the head of 200 uFasimba, he travelled the seventy miles to pay his last respects. Afterwards he travelled a further twenty miles to visit Dingiswayo, when it was decided between the two men that initially they would attack Matiwane's emaNgwaneni, whose clan was positioned amongst the foothills of the Drakensberg range. The attack was scheduled for June, but it is clear that Matiwane had been tipped off that he was to be attacked. As a result, he ordered his non-combatants to scatter and arranged for Mtimkulu's amaHlubi to look after his cattle. The campaign was inconclusive, but Dingiswayo accepted Matiwane's surrender and, much to Shaka's disgust, the target tribe was left largely intact. Paradoxically, it was Mtimkulu's decision to keep Matiwane's cattle which brought matters to a head. Zwide, figuring that Matiwane would be weaker having faced

Dingiswayo and Shaka, and now being without his cattle, annexed his lands and forced the emaNgwaneni out of their territory. This would set in motion a chain reaction which would cause thousands of deaths as tribe-upon-tribe was displaced by landless clans. Ultimately Matiwane's flight would be stopped on 26 July 1828 by Major Dundas. Matiwane would be killed some time later on the orders of Dingane.

Dingiswayo's next logical target was Zwide's Ndwandwe. Dingiswayo and Zwide had been friends, but in 1818 Zwide had murdered Dingiswayo's son-in-law. Dingiswayo's Mtetwa reached the Nwandwe border before Shaka's Zulu. For some inexplicable reason Dingiswayo, unguarded, was captured in Nwandwe territory by one of Zwide's patrols and taken to their kraal, where Zwide ordered his head to be cut off. Zwide then launched his army against the dispirited Mtetwa. It was Shaka's presence which prevented an absolute disaster.

With Dingiswayo's death the entire area was now open to the boldest man to stake his claim. In essence, in addition to Shaka and Zwide, there was one other claimant, being the Qwabes clan. Some Mtetwas had come over to Shaka, notably Ngomane. It was Zwide that moved first against Shaka, precipitating the battle of Kwa Gqokli Hill (emMakhosini Valley) in April 1818.

Battle focus

Kwa Gqokli Hill (emMakhosini Valley)

April 1818

Gqokli Hill stands on the south bank of the White Umfolozi River. Unlike Shaka's usual tactics, he adopted a defensive circular formation on the top of the hill. At the hill's summit was a depression in which Shaka hid some 2,000 men.

It is believed that Shaka's total fighting force was little more than 4,000. Indeed, on the summit he deployed 1,600 men, clearly visible to the enemy, in addition to the 2,000 reserves. Shaka also detached some 700 men to protect the Zulu cattle and act as a decoy.

18

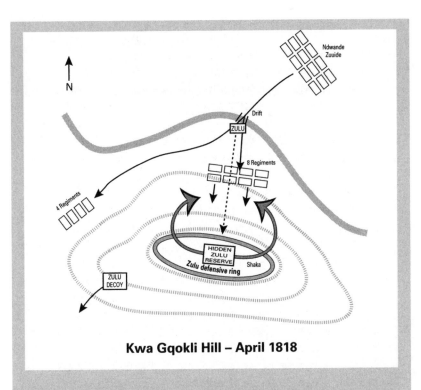

Kwa Gqokli Hill – April 1818

Zwide's force, comprising some 8–10,000 men was organized into twelve regiments. The battle began by the Ndwandwe attempting to force the drifts (fords) across the White Umfolozi. Shaka had posted detachments to deny the crossings and then fall back on his main force, drawing Zwide's Ndwandwe towards him. As the Ndwandwe forced their way across the drifts, Shaka detached the 700 men with the Zulu cattle to draw off some of Zwide's men, effectively reducing the odds facing his army. The ploy worked and Zwide sent four regiments in pursuit of the Zulu cattle.

Meanwhile, eight Ndwandwe regiments (each of around 1,000 men) commanded by Nomahlanjana (Zwide's son and heir) formed up at the foot of Gqokli Hill in preparation for an assault on the summit. At around 09.00 the Ndwandwe regiments began their ascent. As the regiments climbed, the space became more restricted towards the summit. They advanced to within 100 metres, finding all cohesion and order ruined by the terrain. By the time they had closed to 25 metres there was barely room for the Ndwandwe to throw their spears.

As the Ndwandwe hesitated, Shaka threw his troops at their line. It is said that within ten minutes, 1,000 Ndwandwe lay dead and dying around the summit. Nomohlanjana ordered a withdrawl, but Shaka refused to be tempted to abandon his terrain advantage. Shaka deftly replaced the exhausted warriors in the front line with fresh troops and awaited the Ndwandwe's next move.

Nomohlanjana had learned the lesson and realized that his overwhelming numbers would be of no use in this situation. He ordered half of his troops to advance. This time, they would keep the correct intervals and avoid bunching. Again, the Ndwandwe closed to within 25 metres and threw their spears. The Zulu ranks absorbed the barrage, then once again Shaka launched his regiments (his first two lines) against the enemy. After a protracted struggle around the summit Nomohlanjana signalled another withdrawal.

Nomohlanjana now launched the fresh half of his remaining force. He ordered them to close to within 50 metres and then charge. Nomohlanjana proposed to use his superior numbers by deploying reserves from his rear ranks should the Zulu offer any exposed flanks. Unfortunately for the Ndwandwe, as they closed to within 25 metres, Shaka launched his two front lines against them; the Ndwandwe were shaken and forced back. Again the superior numbers of Ndwandwe worked against them as successive ranks tumbled into one another. The Ndwandwe were barely able to defend themselves; the impetus of the Zulu charge, now reinforced by Shaka's third line of defenders, drove them back down the hill.

Nomohlanjana launched two more assault, but both ended in failure. By now it was mid-afternoon and the Ndwandwe were exhausted and thirsty. Many slipped off to find fresh water, whilst Shaka had water supplies secured at the summit.

Nomohlanjana now reasoned that time was running out and that he had to finish the Zulu before nightfall. He detached 1,000 men and placed them in a semi-circle at the southern foot of the hill and then proposed to use the rest of his force to drive Shaka off the hill. The Ndwandwe formed up in a column less than 200 metres wide. Nomohlanjana's plan was simple; the column would force Shaka over the hill and into the waiting arms of 1,000 men and the issue would be settled.

As the Ndwandwe column headed for the summit, Shaka unleashed his carefully husbanded reserves. Two columns (the bull's horns), each of some 750 men, hit the Ndwandwe column's flanks, whilst 500 men stood in reserve (the chest).

The column was shattered and Shaka's troops now circled the hill (bearing in mind that the destination of the column was unknown to the Ndwandwe on the southern foot of the hill). The Ndwandwe's semi-circle broke, but managed to link up with the four regiments that had been detached to chase the Zulu cattle. The Ndwandwe effectives now numbered around 3,500, still outnumbering the exhausted, depleted, yet victorious Zulu. With Zulu in pursuit of the broken column, Shaka could muster around 1,000 men to face the renewed threat.

Shaka retreated towards Kwa Bulawayo, with clusters of Zulu rejoining him along the way. He sent contingents to harry the rear of the advancing Ndwandwe. The Zulu were then grateful to see the Belebele regiment arrive, having dealt with the scattered Ndwandwe seeking water. Shaka directed them to deploy on the right flank of the Ndwandwe and then launched his counter-attack.

It is believed that only 1,000 of the Ndwandwe escaped the encirclement, but those which did, managed to drive the Zulu cattle away with them. The Ndwandwe casualties may well have amounted to some 7,500. Shaka's casualties comparatively were also high, with over 1,500 killed and a further 500 seriously wounded.

By May 1819 Zwide had considerably regrouped and struck again against Shaka, this time leading an army of 18,000 men. The army itself was led by Soshangane. Shaka, too, had not been idle and had raised new regiments and elevated a grandson of Zwide, Mzilakizi, to a position of power in his army, along with Ndlela. Shaka was perfectly aware that Zwide would attempt another invasion. He adopted a scorched earth policy, moving all inhabitants out of a forty-mile belt as far as the Tugela River. The Ndwandwe had learned much from Kwa Gqokli Hill and were now armed with two throwing spears and a short stabbing spear.

The Ndwandwe crossed the White Umfolozi and into Shaka's territory, where they could see Zulu regiments retreating to the south. The Ndwandwe had counted on being able to raid Zulu kraals and obtain additional food, but Shaka's abandonment of the territory denied them this. Over the next four days the Ndwandwe were subjected to raids; even the cattle which they had brought with them had been seized by the Zulu. Soshangane's army was led on a wild goose chase to capture cattle and rations and each time the Ndwandwe was lured further south. Finally Shaka's army began to close and launched a series of coordinated attacks as the Ndwandwe began to retire to the north.

The major engagement probably took place to the east of Sungulweni Hill. The Ndwandwe could muster around 16,000 against Shaka's 10,000 men.

Battle focus

Sungulweni Hill

July 1819

At just under one kilometre Shaka sent two regiments in dense columns to outflank Soshangane's wings, forcing the Ndwandwe to extend their line to prevent themselves from being surrounded. Soshangane detached a regiment from each of his wings to protect against the Zulu encirclement.

Shaka's main body advanced to within 100 metres of the

Ndwandwe line and launched simultaneous attacks on their flanks. He then sent a regiment out on each flank to deal with the two detached Ndwandwe regiments. There was little Soshangane could do to protect these two regiments. The isolated Ndwandwe regiments, although they stubbornly resisted the Zulu, were broken and at this point Shaka broke off the pinning attacks on the flanks of the main Ndwandwe army.

Soshangane ordered his men forward, but each time they advanced, Shaka maintained the same distance between them. Soshangane realized that this was a futile exercise and remaining in battle formation, began to retire. He still had sixteen regiments. Shaka controlled six, but there were four more ahead of the Ndwandwe. The terrain did not favour the Ndwandwe and each time they encountered difficult ground Shaka would nip off the stragglers and slaughter them.

That night Soshangane had reached the Umhaltuze Valley. Shaka positioned his army on a ridge around one kilometre away. In the morning the Ndwandwe, now reduced to around 12,000 men, began to retire across a drift. Soshangane had deployed a strong regiment to cover the crossing. Shaka waited until around half the Ndwandwe had crossed the drift before throwing 7,000 men forward. The Ndwandwe regiments, with the exception of the covering unit, panicked and the Zulu slaughtered hundreds. The covering regiment managed to withdraw in relatively good order.

Shaka was still not satisfied and for some time the hand-to-hand combat ebbed and flowed around the drift. Shaka sent the uFasimba on a wide outflanking movement; these regiments fell on the Ndwandwe. The battles around the Mhlatuze River lasted for around two days; ultimately Soshangane's army disintegrated.

Casualties were enormous and barely half of the Ndwandwe army managed to escape whilst Shaka had lost something in excess of 1,000 men.

Having defeated the Ndwandwe army, it is said that Shaka himself led a fresh reserve the 100 or more kilometres to Zwide's kraal. As the Zulu approached the kraal they were ordered to sing the Ndwandwe victory song. As the Ndwandwe emerged to greet what they thought to be their victorious army, the Zulu fell on them and slaughtered men, women and children. Zwide managed to escape to the north along with his sons but he would die in obscurity. Soshangane would ultimately retreat with the bulk of the remaining Ndwandwe army and form the Shangane nation near St Lucia Bay.

Shaka was now the undisputed owner of 11,500 square miles of territory that stretched from the Pongola River in the north to the Tugela River in the south and from the Blood River in the west to the coast. He could now muster an army of 20,000 men.

Shaka spent a short time consolidating his new gains, but in late 1820 he launched a campaign against the Tembu. He split his army into two flanking divisions; the first tackled the Tembu's allies, the Cunu, led by Macingwane. The Cunu guarded the lower drifts of the Buffalo River. The Tembu themselves, led by Ngosa, guarded the upper drifts, primarily in the region around Mount Hlazakazi.

The Zulu were defeated in battle near the main Tembu kraal, but hundreds of Tembu women and children, not to mention the bulk of their cattle, were captured by the Zulu. The Zulu that had been thrown at the Cunu were no more successful, but both tribes realized that ultimately the Zulu would be victorious and began to head south. Shaka caught up with them in late 1822 and they were scattered to the four winds.

By 1824 Shaka's army was making forays into the Natal area, his men crossing the Tugela River. Shaka's troops encountered virtually no opposition, but one notable encounter near the Opisweni Mountain against the Pepeta clan is worthy of mention. The Pepeta held an all-but impenetrable position at the summit of the mountain. The tribe was led by Mshika and he defied all Zulu attempts to dislodge him. It was virtually impossible for the Zulu to scale the rocky cliffs. The Pepeta had a natural water supply and considerable provisions. Shaka's solution was to construct lengths of rope from cattle hide and assault the summit

24

with men climbing the ropes, protected rather like a Roman testudo. The testudo approached the summit through a gully, whilst Shaka launched diversionary attacks from other directions. The assault was successful and the troops emerged into a gully where, under fire from rocks and spears, they advanced in the tortoise formation. There were some 300 Zulu in the attack facing around 700 Pepeta effectives. Ultimately the Pepeta broke and Shaka's main force was able to mop them up as they fled from the mountain.

Shaka now turned his attention to consolidating his gains and the creation of ever more regiments.

Chapter Three

Shaka's Army

The Zulu army created by Shaka would outlive him and survive until it was destroyed by the British in 1879. As we have seen, warfare before Shaka was a relatively bloodless activity, more related to personal challenges on the battlefield and a symbolic conflict that rarely involved complete destruction of a tribe. The whole nature of Shaka's battlefield tactics irrevocably changed old systems of warfare, placing a greater reliance on hand-to-hand combat. For the first time Shaka, leading an ever-growing Zulu nation, ruthlessly eliminated all rivals and absorbed clan after clan into the nation itself. Power was based upon the size and strength of the army. Each time a tribe was absorbed it was brought into the military system. Setting aside whether Shaka did, or did not, create the assegai and drill his men to fight in ways unknown to the area, it is the way in which he created his army that was his legacy.

Rather than creating regiments made up from potentially disaffected and dissenting conquered tribes, he based his whole recruitment policy on age groups. Men from each tribe would be allocated to an age group and these age groups would then be amalgamated into a regiment, regardless of their tribal background. This created the cohesion and allegiance to the regiment, rather than to the tribe. Potentially at least, every man who had reached the age of eighteen was liable to be called up into the army. Each of the various age groups, or amabutho, would be allocated to a specific regiment and would undergo training at an ikhanda.

Effectively once the men had been called up to their regimental barracks they were under the direct control of the king. This served a dual purpose; not only were the able-bodied fighting men out of the control of the tribal chieftains, but they also provided the king with a vast labour pool. It was a centralizing system which instilled national spirit, as opposed to local allegiances. Shaka retained control of these men until many of them were almost forty years old. At this point the regiment would be allowed to marry. Once this had taken place the men effectively became reservists, liable to be called up if the king decided it was necessary.

Women, too, were required to be members of an amabutho and ultimately, when a male regiment was deemed ready for marriage, all of the brides were chosen from a matched female amabutho. This did, of course, mean in the majority of cases that the women were considerably younger than their husbands. Yet marriage and hence the children created in that marriage were the sons and daughters of men who had survived and proved themselves in battle. In some respects, therefore, the system adopted by Shaka was rather like a process of natural selection in that only the strongest, fittest and bravest men would produce children.

There is considerable debate as to how many effective fighting men Shaka could call upon. It is possible that the core of his army, consisting of around fifteen regiments, would have mustered around 14,000 men. In addition to this number there were older men who could be considered as reservists, plus several semi-autonomous tribes who contributed men as and when required. By the time the British clashed with the Zulu in 1879, Cetshwayo had around thirty-four regiments and possibly as many as 42,000 men. This figure includes many men, again reservists, who were of advancing years and of limited value. A more accurate figure for Cetshwayo's effective army strength is something in excess of 25,000 men.

In creating a centralized society Shaka and his successors needed a highly hierarchical structure. At tribal level the izikhulu, or local chieftain, acted on behalf of, and in the name of, the king. The izikhulu had the power to summarily execute those who had infringed the law. Lesser crimes were dealt with by the confiscation of cattle.

At the age of four or five years a young Zulu boy would effectively begin his military training. This would commence with the responsibility of looking after sheep, goats and calves. The boys would carry a stick rather than a spear and in addition to their herding responsibilities, they would also hunt with dogs. Stick fighting was encouraged and the head was the main target in these fights. Small game would be killed by throwing the stick. By the time the boy had reached the age of eleven or twelve he would be sharing a hut with several boys of his own age and would now have the primary responsibility of looking after the cattle. At the age of about fifteen years old the boy would become an udibi and would be responsible for carrying his father's or elder brother's gourd, blankets, headrest and sleeping mat for journeys, and possibly into battle. The boy's first experience of the regimental system would be when he accompanied his father or an elder brother to an ikhanda. He could spend several weeks here, learning the daily rituals and activities of the regiment.

At the age of around sixteen or seventeen the boys would report to an ikhanda of their own. The boys were organized into companies, known as iviyo, between 50 and 200 strong. The boys' principle source of food was milk from the cattle. On their arrival they would perform ukukleza, which meant to drink the milk straight from the cattle's udder. They were, in effect, accepting the protection and sustenance of the king in return for their service. The boys would remain as cadets for around two to four years. Natural leaders would emerge. They would be used for general labouring duties and agricultural work and learn the basics of fighting with sticks. They did not, at this point, carry spears. After this period it would be decided that there were enough boys regionally to form a regiment and they would be called to the king's kraal to be enrolled.

The process was simple; the king would greet them, name the regiment and instruct them to build a new ikhanda nearby which would then become the regimental headquarters. Once the military kraal had been built, the cadets could now expect to be called up for training at the kraal for several months of each year. They would not just be trained, but would also be required to carry out any labouring work ordered by the king. Once the regiment had been created, the king would appoint two induna, or officers, to command the regiment. Effectively they would control the regiment on behalf of the king, again adding to the centralized authority of the nation. The vast majority of induna would be drawn from families who had strong links with the king himself. They would tend to be men who already had military experience, having served in an existing regiment. Each of the iviyo within a regiment also had an officer. Sometimes they were men who had naturally risen from the ranks, or those who had caught an induna, or even the king's eye. There does not appear to have been a hard and fast system, either in the appointments of indunas, or iviyo officers; some were simply friends of the king, others were men who had proved themselves in battle; some were minor chieftains in their own right, whilst others appear to simply be political appointments.

Within the regimental kraal the men would live four or five to a hut, with a requisite number of udibi boys to look after them. Dancing appears to have been one of the many ways in which the Zulu learned to move in formation. Dancing itself was highly ritualized, with movement in formation backwards and forwards often accompanied by the beating of shields with sticks. The men were taught how to take up position in ranks, how to charge and ultimately how to use the shield and the spear together for hand-to-hand fighting. The king provided the food, primarily boiled grain, porridge, occasionally meat and beer. In reality, however, the king only ever provided the meat and beer; all other foodstuffs had to be provided by the families of the warriors. The meat was provided by slaughtering cattle from the royal herd.

Marriage was not allowed until the men had given at least fifteen years of service, by which time they were in their late thirties. Bearing in mind that the king had virtual control over the regiment until such a time as the men married, the monarch was often reluctant to allow marriage until the latest possible opportunity.

The most potent symbol for the Zulu army was the shield. War shields belonged to the king, but the Zulu used the shield for a variety of other purposes. A tiny shield, known as the umgabelo-munye, was used for dancing. The igqoka was used for courting and a man's personal shield, rather than his war shield, was known as the ihawu. The Zulu war shields were called isihlangu, which means to brush aside. They would vary in size from approximately 2 metres tall by 1 metre across to a more regular 1.5 metres tall by just under 1 metre wide. In terms of hand-to-hand fighting, obviously the larger the shield, the more protection it provided the warrior. From around the time of the Zulu civil war in the 1850s, a smaller shield, which would be the most common carried by the Zulu army in 1879, had been introduced. This was known as the umbumbuluzo and it was considerably smaller than the standard war shield, somewhat more rounded and lighter. All of the shields were created from cow hide. Typically, the cattle would be skinned and the hide cleaned and prepared. It would then be buried for several days. The hair would be retained in order to provide the distinctive colouring of the shield for the regiment. The hide itself was pliable and it was possible to roll up the shield after dismantling it for storage or easier transportation. Experienced shield makers would cut the basic shape and then make a series of parallel slits in the centre, through which strips of hide would be threaded. This would serve a dual purpose; firstly it strengthened the centre of the shield and also allowed the shield stick to be fastened to the hide. The shield stick extended along the length of the shield, on the top of which animal skin would be bound. The bottom of the shield stick was sharpened and it could be used to stab the legs of an enemy in combat. Normally the strips of hide which were threaded into the shield were of a contrasting colour. The slits were known as amagabelo and were usually spaced one or two inches from each other.

When a regiment was to be given their shields, the king's cattle would be sorted by colour, and animals of a similar colour would be selected for slaughter. The king would also require his chieftains to provide cattle of particular colours in order to supplement the supply. Generally speaking, younger regiments would be provided with predominantly black shields. The Zulu believed that black inferred youth and strength. Whiter cattle and shields were reserved for more senior regiments, as white and grey inferred wisdom. After Shaka, and particularly during the reign of Cetshwayo, red shields and white shields became associated with married regiments. Darker shields were known as insane, red shields with white spots known as imitshezi, whilst black shields with white spots were called nkone.

Prior to the British invasion in 1879 a comprehensive listing of the Zulu regiments identified them by noting the colour of the shields. However, it appears that by 1879 much of the more formal shield colour identification had passed from popularity. It should be borne in mind that the Zulu had considerably less cattle by the 1870s than they had in the past. It was becoming common practice for the king to provide buffalo meat, rather than meat from his herds, to feed the regiments. Equally, in order to secure firearms by the 1870s the Zulu was exporting tens of thousands of hides, which again reduced the available stock. It is presumed that as the regiment gained seniority its shields would become increasingly white. There may have been very practical reasons for this occurrence, since a shield was unlikely to be of serviceable value after four or five years. This would mean that any warrior would have three or four shields even before he became a married man.

As already noted, Shaka was credited with having effectively banned the use of the throwing spear. It is argued that he believed that throwing spears at the enemy was in essence a cowardly act and that a true warrior needed to prove himself in hand-to-hand combat. The warrior would have no excuse to avoid closing with the enemy; in order to kill he had to face his enemy at close quarters. There is some evidence, however, that after Shaka's death many Zulu warriors carried at least one throwing spear, in addition to their stabbing spear.

Zulu metalwork was comparatively primitive, yet the stabbing spear, which had a blade some 45 centimetres long and 4 centimetres wide, was made of molten ore mixed with charcoal. The blade was fixed to the wooden shaft (uti) with vegetable glue. Strips of bark would be bound around the socket and then covered with hide taken from a cow's tail. The stabbing spear, including the shaft, was around 1 metre long. The wooden shaft was thicker at the opposite end to the blade in order to help prevent the spear from slipping out of the man's hand as he pulled it out of a stabbed enemy. The stabbing spear, commonly known as the assegai, is also known as the iklwa, which is a word said to describe the sound of the spear being pulled from flesh. The stabbing spear carried by the warriors in 1879 was somewhat different; the ntlekwane had a blade around 30 centimetres long and only 3 centimetres wide.

It is unclear whether the assegais were made-to-measure for each warrior. In other words it is uncertain whether the warriors commissioned a metalworker to make an assegai, or whether the metalworkers supplied assegais in bulk to the king, who then distributed them to the regiment. In any case, the assegai was the personal possession of the warrior, unlike the shield which technically belonged to the king. There is some evidence that many of the men had assegais and throwing spears made for them and there is further evidence to suggest that a goat would be reasonable recompense for two spears.

The stabbing spear was designed to be used underarm and was equally intended to be used in conjunction with the shield in an offensive manner. Again Shaka is credited with showing his contemporaries how to use the heavier bladed assegai in conjunction with the shield. Typically, a Zulu warrior would either bash their opponent with their shield, knocking him off balance in order to deliver a thrust with his assegai, or, more effectively, to hook the opponent's shield, pulling him off balance and exposing his chest to the thrust. Throwing spears, when carried, were held by the shield hand. They had an effective range of no more than about 30 metres, although the Zulu would throw their spears at anything up to 50 metres distant. The shaft of a throwing spear was approximately 1 metre long.

Not all Zulu warriors were armed with an assegai or throwing spear. Some were armed with the iwisa or knobkerrie, which was effectively a war club. Typically, these would be just over half a metre long, with a head between 10 and 18 centimetres across. Some had metal studs hammered into the head for additional impact. Some Zulu carried the isizenze, or battleaxe, although it may have been the case that this was more a ceremonial weapon. The isizenze was used to chop and commonly had a half-moon blade.

For the majority of time a warrior would wear nothing more

than a box made of grass and banana leaves for privacy. This was known as the umcedo. Sometimes he would wear strips of hide around his waist, known as an umutsha; the front was known as the isinene and the back the ibeshu. The animal skins would usually not extend far below the warrior's buttocks. The quality of the skins would be an indication as to the seniority and rank of the man wearing them. When a regiment was mustered, the men would wear more ornate skins over their basic ones, which would give the impression that they were wearing a kilt.

Married men tended to wear otter skins sewn into a roll tied to the back of their heads as their principle headdress, known as an umqele. Unmarried warriors would wear leopard skin. Monkey skin would be sewn to the headband and these would drape over the ears to the jaw line. Younger regiments would wear the tail feathers of the isakabuli (widow bird) tied to porcupine quills or dried grass. Other regiments would use ostrich feathers, predominantly those of black and white. More senior men would wear the tail feathers of the blue crane (indwe); a handful would also wear eagle feathers. The skin and hair from cattle tails would be wrapped around the upper arm, usually just above the elbow and also above the knees. On occasion they would also be worn around the ankles and wrists. Other cattle tails would be sewn to a necklace of hide which was worn around the waist like a belt. It seems that skins and pelts from leopards, otters, monkeys and other wild animals were often provided directly to the Zulu king as tribute from lesser tribes.

When ceremonial costumes were not being worn they would be stored in protective bundles and were carried to a muster by udibi boys. It was for the king to determine which regiments were entitled to wear leopard skins. Indeed leopard skin pelts and pelts from lions were the property of the king; it was for him to choose whether a regiment was entitled to wear hide from these animals. This was also the case for certain feathers, such as the iGwalagwala (scarlet lourie). These feathers were restricted to those who had a royal connection by birth.

The ceremonial costumes were used only during ceremonies; it was impractical to wear such ornate costume in battle. The umKhosi was an annual event prior to the harvest to celebrate the power and the wealth of the king and the Zulu nation. Again it was used as a centralizing and unifying occasion. The entire army would be mustered and required to attend the ceremony at the king's principle kraal. No Zulu would dare to harvest his crops prior to this ceremony. The precise timing of the ceremony was dependent upon the ripeness of gourds. Gourds were collected from various parts of the kingdom and examined to discover how close to ripening they were. It was only when they were ready that the king would begin to prepare himself for the ceremony. In terms of the army's responsibilities at ceremonies such as these, a select number of members of a particular regiment would be required to kill a black bull with their bare hands. It was not always the case that the entire army was mustered for such ceremonies. In fact it was common for only the local regiments to be required to attend; the unmarried warriors were chosen to represent the army.

The flesh of the slaughtered bull would be fed to the udibi boys. The internal organs would be used to create purifying potions which would later be used on the eve of the army leaving to under-take a campaign. The umKhosi usually took place towards the end of December or the beginning of January each year. The repre-sentatives of the selected regiments would attend in full regalia. It would begin by the army parading. The regiments would take up positions in order of seniority, with the more senior regiments nearest the king's quarters and the younger regiments further away, near the main gate of the kraal. After again checking the gourds, the bull would now be slaughtered and the internal organs and the ash from the fire on which the bull had been cooked were collected and added to the inkatha. The inkatha was essentially a coil of grass rope which represented the force that held the nation together. At this stage the king would be wearing a costume made of reeds and on the second day he would make his way to a river, where he would have a purifying bath. This would wash away the medicines and potions which he had daubed on his body throughout the ceremony. His reed costume was then burned. The king's bath would be followed by the warriors bathing in the same river and the ceremony would end with the king granting the right to marry to selected regiments.

The last Zulu umKhosi took place over the winter of 1877–8,

due to the fact that war was becoming increasingly inevitable by the time the ceremony should have taken place over the Christmas and New Year period of 1878–9.

It was vitally important for the king to ensure that his army was spiritually prepared for battle. In some respects this doctoring, as it was known, bore similarities with the umKhosi ceremony. The purpose of the doctoring was to ritually purify the army and to bind them together in a common purpose. The king would summon the nation's most senior doctors; each man would be given medicine to swallow, which he was then required to vomit out into a hole some 2 metres deep. The medicine itself was designed to assist the warriors in vomiting and once each regiment had vomited into its hole, a sample was taken which would be added to the inkatha. The hole would then be filled in and extreme measures would be taken to ensure that the location of the hole remained a secret. The regiment would then march to the king's kraal, where a black bull would be killed by hand. The flesh of the bull was roasted and the army would take up position in a circle. Strips of the cooked meat were thrown into the crowd; the warriors would grab the chunks of meat, take a bite and then throw it behind them for other men. Each man would chew his piece of meat, swallowing the juice but spitting out the remains. If a piece of meat fell on the ground it would have lost its purifying strength. Having gone through this ritual, the men were now considered to be spiritually prepared for battle. Until such a time as the men had fought in battle, they were banned from any contact with women, including the consumption of any food prepared by women.

The troops now had supernatural strength called ithonya. Theoretically this would ensure that they were victorious in battle; however, their supernatural powers may be inferior to those of their enemies. Assuming that the troops were about to be thrown into battle, the king would now require two named regiments to challenge one another. This was known as xoxa and was designed to further enhance their aggressiveness and rivalry. It was normally the case that similarly aged regiments would be pitted against one another. The two regiments would face one another and challenges would be made. Physical conflict did not take place but the challengers shadow fought one another and generally whipped up battle frenzy.

The final act before the regiments went off to battle involved creating a concoction of roots and plants. An oxtail was dipped into the medicine and the potion was then sprinkled over the warriors. It is possible that body parts from enemies were used in this potion, as may have been the case directly after the battle of Italeni, which is one explanation as to the disappearance of the body of Dirkie Uys. There may have been at least one other instance of this when the bodies of three white men were discovered after a skirmish on 3 July 1879 near the White Umfolozi River. Their bodies had been mutilated and it is perfectly possible that their noses and hearts, amongst other things, were used in the purification ceremony which took place that night. Much later, in 1906, the body of Sergeant Brown of the Natal Mounted Police was found to be missing his upper lip and other body parts; it is believed that Bambatha's doctors had used them for their purification ceremony.

Unless the king himself had decided to accompany the army on campaign, which was generally rare, the army would now be in the hands of selected induna. By choice the Zulu army would tend to carry out their campaigns between June and August. These were the winter months, when the weather was cooler and the harvest had already been gathered. It was for this reason amongst many others that the British chose January, at the beginning of the harvest, to launch their invasion. At this stage of the year food stocks would be low.

Probably in the earlier years many of the Zulu marched into battle with most of their ceremonial regalia. It is unlikely they actually wore it on the battlefield. On the eve of the conflict their ceremonial regalia would be rolled up in their sleeping mats and would then become the responsibility of the udibi boys. It tended to be the case that the younger men wore very little into battle, whilst more senior men might retain some skins or tails and, perhaps, cow tails tied around their limbs. The vast majority of the men would wear necklaces which had blocks of willow wood in a pouch. A large number would also carry snuff which, at the very least, would help stave off hunger in a protracted battle.

The king's favourite young regiment would lead the army. It is probable that on average the army would cover some twenty miles per day. The induna, in overall command of the force, would seek to ensure that the army was not physically exhausted before it reached the battlefield. Bearing in mind that the army ran barefoot at all times, this is still a staggering feat, given the difficult terrain in which the army operated. On campaign the men would be sustained by what they could carry themselves and what they could reasonably expect an udibi boy to carry. For the most part they lived off the land, but Zulu kraals would be expected to contribute if the army passed their way. Inside enemy territory they would help themselves to whatever food was available. Given the fact that thousands of cattle would be seized in a major campaign, there was never any significant shortage of food. Traditionally the Zulu would eat in the middle of the morning and in the early evening. Therefore if a battle was to take place at early light they would not have eaten since dusk on the previous day.

In friendly territory the army would proceed in a single column, but once it neared enemy territory or an enemy force, it would split into two groups, each commanded by an induna. At all times the army was preceded by a screen of scouts. In between the scouts was a screen of skirmishers which was drawn from various regiments to effectively screen the army and deal with enemy scouts and foragers. It was just such a screen of skirmishers which fooled Chelmsford, in January 1879, to draw off half of his force in pursuit, believing it to be the main Zulu army. It was also the skirmishers which dealt with Russell's rocket battery at Isandlwana. The Prince Imperial, too, was killed by skirmishers on 1 June 1879.

Having now arrived within striking distance of the enemy, a final ritual was undertaken, where once again the warriors would be sprinkled with medicines. The induna would now urge the men to do their utmost for the king and the nation. The troops would be drawn up into four major groupings, representing the two horns, the chest or centre of the army and the reserves. The latter group would then be deployed either in support of the centre or to exploit success either on the left or the right.

In the light of what we do know about the 1879 campaign, it

begins to become abundantly obvious that whilst the bull's horn tactic was a tried and trusted means of imposing the Zulu will on the battlefield, it was rarely coordinated. In theory, the head of the army, its centre, would steadily advance towards the enemy. It had a dual purpose; first it would physically pin the bulk of the enemy in a position where it would have to face the oncoming threat and, secondly, it would attract their attention, allowing the two horns to fan out left and right in an attempt to get around the back of the enemy force. These series of movements required close co-ordination. Since the horns would invariably be made up of younger men, far more eager for battle than the more senior men in the centre, there was every chance that the horns would precipitate early contact with the enemy. Added to this, it was not always possible, due to terrain restrictions, to coordinate both of the horns or to ensure that they were in place before the chest closed with the enemy. On several occasions during 1879 the British successfully goaded the horns into making premature attacks before the rest of the army was in place. Equally, at Ncome River in 1838, successive waves of brave, yet uncoordinated regiments attempted to close with the Voortrekker's laager to no great effect. In many respects the Zulu horn formation and mode of attack relied on the Zulu maintaining the initiative. They hoped that the formation would catch the enemy off guard and that in seeing Zulu regiments surge around their flanks and appear in their rear, they would be psychologically undermined.

Traditionally laid out and deployed enemy often fell into this trap. It could be argued that the British at Isandlwana were guilty of making this mistake. However, more mobile, or compact enemy would be unperturbed by the flanking moves of the Zulu. British squares, for example, would be able to deliver stinging defensive fire from any direction. This is equally the case for a well positioned Boer laager. Indeed the Zulu had absolutely no answer to an enemy in prepared positions, as could be seen at Rorke's Drift and at Eshowe.

The enemy could at least be assured of the fact that the Zulu were unlikely to attack during the hours of darkness. The Zulu only continued to engage the British forces at Rorke's Drift on the assumption that they were about to overrun the garrison.

Not only were the problems of coordination compounded by darkness, but the Zulu also believed that the army would be vulnerable to evil supernatural powers if they fought at night.

As we have seen, the preferred tactic of encirclement, known as impondo zankomo, used four distinct groups of regiments. The chest itself, known as the isifuba, would advance directly on the enemy. The encircling horns, known as izimpondo, would normally consist of the younger, more fleet-footed men. The loins, or reserves, known as the umuva, were designed to be thrown into battle wherever they were needed. In many cases the reserves were kept out of sight of the battlefield for fear that they would make a pre-emptory attack without orders. In some cases the Zulu army would also have an isibiba which literally meant those that remained behind. These men would tend to be the most recent regiments mustered, with little or no combat experience. The isibiba could be unleashed on the enemy once he had been broken and used to seize any enemy cattle in the area.

In cases when the Zulu tactic failed it was either as a result of a lack of coordination between the four elements of the army, either because of impetuous charges or difficult terrain, or the fact that the army had underestimated the firepower of a particular element of the enemy force. In the latter cases, encircling movements were stopped dead in their tracks and the rest of the army closed with the enemy without the benefit of the threat of the horn which had failed to secure its position. Even in smaller battles a regiment, or a number of companies of a regiment, would automatically adopt the beast's horn formation.

The beast's head tactics had primarily been developed to deal with armies that fought on foot. The tactics had to be adapted in order to deal with mounted troops, such as the Boers. Invariably the Zulu would use ambush tactics to deal with cavalry. Commonly a cattle herd was driven to within sight of the enemy. The Zulu warriors would hide behind ridges or in long grass. At the battle of Italeni in 1838 this tactic worked perfectly and the Boers were drawn into an ambush and nearly became surrounded and slaughtered. A similar tactic was used by the abaQulusi at Hlobane. Shortly before the battle of Ulundi in 1879 Buller's cavalry were nearly lured into an area which had been well prepared by the Zulu. They had plaited the grass to trip the horses and on either side of the area the Zulu warriors lay in wait. Unfortunately for the Zulu the uMxapho regiment charged prematurely and the British troopers were able to escape the trap.

In a conventional battle both the chest and the horns would move at speed in open order, preceded by skirmishers. They would move at the jog. If the men had firearms they would begin to open fire at around 800 metres, otherwise they would seek to close with the enemy in these lines as quickly as possible. As the Zulu closed on their enemy, the formations would close into more compact lines and they would accelerate into a run. Throwing spears would be cast at around 30 metres; seconds later the front line of the Zulu regiment would impact upon the enemy. During the war in 1879 the Zulu occasionally fired volleys with their muskets and rifles prior to charging, but since the majority of the weapons were muzzle loaders, it is probable that only one shot was fired before the charge went in.

The vast majority of the muskets owned by the Zulu were obsolete weapons, with an effective range of no more than 100 metres. In effect, the muskets were used in a similar way to the throwing spear. It is also the case that many of the Zulu were reluctant to use muskets in the conventional manner. They were notoriously poor shots and would often fire the musket at arm's length in order to avoid the recoil on their shoulder. It was only after Isandlwana that the Zulu army had access to modern weapons. They captured upwards of 1,000 Martini-Henry rifles and over half a million rounds of ammunition. Even then many of the rounds were cannibalized so that the powder could be used for the men's muzzle loading rifles. In any event, whilst the throwing spear was considered a cowardly way of fighting the enemy, the rifle was considered doubly so because of the range at which one could engage the enemy.

The Zulu induna on the battlefield would invariably try to find a hill from which they would be able to view the whole of the battle and pass directions to regimental induna as events developed. Signals would be used to direct the regiments, but more commonly messengers would be sent from the induna to the regiment. Interestingly, regimental induna were expected to lead their unit from the front, as was the case at Rorke's Drift, when Dabulamanzi kaMpande led the attack, a feat he would repeat at Gingindlovu (where he was wounded). Regiments which faltered on the battlefield were verbally chastised and goaded into making further attacks by their induna. They were often reminded that signs of cowardice would be exploited by a rival regiment.

Prior to facing disciplined fire from the British, and to a lesser extent from the Boer, Zulu casualties in traditional warfare would be light until hand-to-hand combat. When they faced the British they could expect artillery fire at 3,000 metres, but particularly galling was the rifle fire at around 800 metres; it was particularly devastating at half that range. The Zulu captured at least one British artillery piece at Isandlwana, but they could not fathom how it worked.

Time after time against both the Boers and the British, the ill-protected Zulu warriors were subjected to devastating firepower. Certainly adrenalin and, to a large extent, the purification ceremonies, had a great deal to do with the ferocity and certainty of the Zulu in battle. In recent years it has also been suggested that mixed in with the tobacco was cannabis. This was taken as snuff which would not only have fended off hunger, but also have left the men somewhat more impervious to pain and tiredness. It has also been suggested that hallucinogenic drugs were mixed in with the snuff which, to some extent, explains the blood lust.

At the end of a battle, assuming that the Zulu controlled the field, it was imperative that the enemy dead were ritually mutilated. This took the shape of a slash in the abdomen, known as qaqa. This would allow the spirit of the dead man to escape; otherwise the killer of the man would suffer from umnyama, a madness which would cause his body to expand. It was also common practice for the victorious warrior to take some clothing from the dead man.

For the wounded Zulu, medical attention was somewhat rudimentary. Broken bones would have splints bound to them and wounds would be treated with a handful of grass pushed into the flesh at the point of impact. Zulu doctors were perfectly capable of dealing with many wounds; they would be cleaned and sewn up. Herbal remedies were often used to deal with infected wounds.

41

Warriors who had received wounds which appeared to be ulti-mately fatal would be dispatched with a swift spear thrust to the heart. The Zulu dead tended not to be buried; they were simply covered by their shields. In some cases the bodies would be dragged into a donga, but more often than not they would be left where they had fallen.

The men who had survived the battle now had to be purified once more. They could not undertake normal activities until this process had been completed. Those who had killed an enemy were known as izinxweleha and were separated from the rest of the people for at least four or five days. They proceeded to a river, where they would have a ritual bath. They would be given medi-cines and effectively re-purified. The regiments would then be summoned to the king, where further purification ceremonies took place. The izinxweleha would wear asparagus in their hair during these ceremonies, where the regimental induna would describe the actions of the regiment to the king. The izinxweleha would then be given a willow stick which they would cut up and have threaded into their necklaces, which were known as iziqu. Those men who had particularly distinguished themselves in battle would be given bronze armbands (izingxotha).

In traditional tribal warfare cattle would have been taken from the enemy. The vast majority of these animals would become part of the royal herd, although some would be given to members of the regiment. Particularly brave men would be given up to ten cattle. Any other items which had been taken during or after the battle were the personal property of the warriors concerned. Men, who had shown cowardice on the battlefield, at least in the early years, would be slaughtered, particularly during the reign of Shaka. In any event cowards were always treated with contempt and publicly humiliated. Married men who had shown themselves to be cowards would often have their wedding bands removed.

With a few notable exceptions, up until 1879 the Zulu had tasted victory on more occasions than they had suffered defeats. Time after time during the 1879 conflict the Zulu fought them-selves to a standstill, attacking again and again until they were exhausted or decimated. Neither the indunas nor the warriors, were overly keen on reporting failure to their king. By the battle of Ulundi in July 1879 it was abundantly clear to Cetshwayo, his indunas and warriors that the war was virtually lost. Nonetheless the army mustered for one last time and were subsequently roughly handled by Chelmsford's men. Shortly after the battle, Cetshwayo himself fled and there was virtually no resistance. Zulu casualties during the 1879 war alone may have exceeded 10,000 men.

The strategy and tactics which had served the Zulu so well for over fifty years had ultimately floundered in the face of disciplined and destructive firepower. The regimental system was stripped away, and from that point on factions comprising the armies that would fight in numerous later engagements, became more tribally based and much less like Shaka's creation.

Chapter Four

Mzilikazi's Matabele

Mzilikazi was born in 1790, the son of Mashobane and his Ndwandwe wife called Monpethu. Mashobane was chieftain of a northern tribe of the Khumalo, lying between the esiKwebesi and the umKuze Rivers.

As heir to his father's kingdom, Mzilikazi and his mother were sent to Zwide's royal kraal. Zwide, Mzilikazi's grandfather, watched Dingiswayo's Mthethwa clan gradually grow in prominence, annexing the lands of innumerable tribes, as his dominance of the region grew. Zwide, too, was increasing his area of influence and took full advantage in incorporating tribes which had already been subjugated by Dingiswayo. By 1818, with Shaka as an able lieutenant, Dingiswayo controlled much of the land to the south of the Black Umfolozi. Inevitably Zwide's and Dingiswayo's ambitions would collide.

Dingiswayo moved first and as we have seen he led his army into Zwide's country, only to be captured unguarded and murdered by Zwide. It would appear that Donda, Mzilikazi's cousin, warned Shaka of what had happened to Dingiswayo and, in retribution, Zwide ordered Donda's clan to be eliminated. Donda was chieftain of the southern Khumalo and Zwide's warriors ruthlessly eliminated the tribe, murdering Donda, his heir and Mashobane, Mzilikazi's father. From that point on Mzilikazi hated Zwide. Nonetheless, Zwide appointed Mzilikazi as chieftain of his father's tribe and later in the year the Ndwandwe were beaten by Shaka at kwa Qokli hill. Mzilikazi realized the way the wind was blowing and crossed the White Umfolozi, offering both his services and that of his tribe to Shaka.

Shaka welcomed him with open arms and he fought in his first campaign against the Ndwandwe during their second invasion of Shaka's empire. It was here he first impressed Shaka and he began to be brought into the close circle of Shaka's advisors. In June 1822 Mzilikazi was rewarded with his first independent command; he would lead a Zulu expeditionary force against the Usuthu to the north-west. At the head of two regiments he led his predominantly Khumalo warriors across the White Umfolozi and into the area near the Ngome forest. It was familiar territory and with relative ease he scattered the Usuthu and rounded up their cattle, bringing them back to his former kraal.

Mzilikazi now faced a difficult decision; Shaka would expect him to send all of the captured cattle back to his kraal. He knew that if he defied Shaka then his life was forfeit and instead he chose to gather up his tribe and march into the esiKwebezi valley, hoping that any force which Shaka sent after him could be dealt with. It was not long afterwards that Shaka did indeed send a punitive expedition to capture Mzilikazi, but by now Mzilikazi had taken up a strong position on a hill, known as enTubeni. The Zulu made two attempts to storm the position, but each time they were thrown back in disorder. Ultimately they gave up and headed back to Shaka's kraal to tell him the bad news.

Surprisingly Shaka seems to have been somewhat proud of his protégé and his rough handling of the Zulu regiments, but perhaps in order to avoid losing face, he ordered a second attempt to deal with Mzilikazi. More Zulu regiments arrived in the region towards the beginning of 1823. Again it began to appear that the expedition would be unsuccessful, but Mzilikazi's half-brother, Nzeni, surrendered himself and offered to lead the Zulu along a secret pass around Mzilikazi's position. While Zulu units held Mzilikazi's attention by appearing to be preparing for a frontal assault, the bulk of the Zulu force managed to work its way onto the summit of the hill, where they managed to scatter most of the Khumalo.

Having dealt with the bulk of Mzilikazi's force, the Zulu now turned for home. What remained of the Khumalo rallied and

Mzilikazi led them into Nyoka's territory. He and his tribe would offer no assistance for fear that the Zulu would slaughter them out of hand. Fearing that Nyoka would inform Shaka, Mzilikazi scattered his emaNgweni clan, took their cattle and stored grain and continued his march north.

Mzilikazi's clan, with little more than 300 warriors, were now deep in Usuthu territory. They struck terror into the local tribes and became known as the abakwaZulu (the people of Zululand). Mzilikazi established a temporary kraal in what would become known as the Ermelo district of South Africa. From here he ranged far and wide, gathering cattle and attacking kraals. Mzilikazi followed Shaka's policy of incorporation and recruited many Usuthu warriors into his own army.

After winning a major engagement against the Maphuthing and the Nyawo, led by Sembane, Mzilikazi continued on his northern trek. By 1824 he had reached the sub-tropical area which would later become known as the Middelburg. Here he decided to establish his royal kraal, which became known as ekuPumuleni (the place of rest). Again Mzilikazi followed Shaka's pattern of military establishment, creating regimental kraals and incorporating local tribes into his army.

Once again a handful of local tribes sought to ally themselves against Mzilikazi; this time they were led by Mokotoko and Sibindi. The two chieftains adopted a novel tactic to deal with Mzilikazi's army, stampeding a herd of cattle directly at the Khumalo, with their warriors following up behind. At the crucial moment the stampeding cattle swerved away and were then driven straight back towards the Usuthu. In the ensuing chaos, although the two chieftains and many of the non-combatants escaped, their army was slaughtered. Ultimately Mokotoko was captured and impaled.

Shortly before this, Mzilikazi had led an expedition against another Usuthu tribe, the Bapedi, led by Sekwata. Here they had encountered a more steadfast opposition, as the Bapedi occupied almost impregnable mountain kraals. The attacks on the mountain strongholds were a failure, but Mzilikazi vowed to return and deal with Sekwata at a later date.

Towards the end of 1825 Mzilikazi decided to abandon

ekuPumuleni and head west. He was bound for the territory owned by the Bakwena, said to be the most prosperous of the Usuthu. Their territory lay between the Magaliesberg Mountains and the Limpopo River. It was around this time that Mzilikazi's people began to be called the Matabele, tebele meaning sinking out of sight, referring to the fact that the Khumalo hid behind their huge ox hide shields in battle. Within a relatively short period of time, the whole of the Bakwena territory had been subjugated. It was certainly achieved by early 1826 and Mzilikazi's Matabele was now a powerful and prosperous tribe. Mzilikazi now set about establishing permanent kraals and military barracks across the whole region. During this time Mzilikazi welcomed and incorporated scattered groups of Ndwandwe warriors who had fled from their own territory, following Shaka's defeat of Zwide.

Towards the end of 1826 Mzilikazi sent five regiments to reconnoitre the territory owned by the Mashona. This was a tribe rich in cattle and led by Mgibe, and his kraal, Makhwarane, would obviously be the primary target. It was also around this time that a second campaign was launched against the Bapedi; this time the assaults were successful and the prisoners were brought back to Mzilikazi's royal kraal at emHlahlandlela, being used as slaves to extend the facility.

The successes of Mzilikazi and his cattle wealth drew the attention of the Bergenaars, who were a nomadic group of cattle raiders. They traded cattle for firearms and ammunition, spoke Dutch, they were mounted and wore European clothes. They began raiding the extremities of Mzilikazi's kingdom, but always managed to evade the Matabele before an army could be deployed against them. By the end of 1827, however, the Bergenaars, led by Jan Bloem, along with the Bataung and the Barolong tribes, had mustered to invade the Matabele's land. The allied army began attacking outlying Matabele kraals and managed to appropriate hundreds of cattle. As it transpired, after just a couple of days, the army had rounded up enough cattle and withdrew. They were certain that Mzilikazi could not be in a position to do anything about their raids, yet as dusk fell the Matabele began closing on Bloem's force. Unlike the Zulu, the Matabele launched a night attack and scattered the army. The cattle were recovered and to Mzilikazi's delight they had also captured a number of muskets. The Matabele army set off in pursuit of the fleeing enemy and one column marched as far as the Orange River. Here it encountered a Boer commando. The Matabele launched two attacks against the Boers which ended in failure and consequently they returned home. This was to be the first encounter of many between the Matabele and the Boer.

Mzilikazi heard word of Shaka's death in December 1828. He was not to know at that time that Shaka's successor, Dingane, would become one of his most implacable enemies.

Meanwhile, Moletsane's Bataung, had fallen out with the Barolong tribe and the latter turned to Mzilikazi for protection. At around the same time Mzilikazi had established trading relations with Robert Schoon and William McLuckie in order to secure muskets and ammunition. Mzilikazi was true to his word and his Matabele fell on Moletsane's army and slaughtered them.

By July 1829 Schoon and McLuckie were encamped outside of Mzilikazi's enKungwini kraal. Whilst negotiations were underway, the Europeans learned that Mzilikazi had managed to ambush some of Jan Bloem's bandits and had seized a number of their muskets. Shortly afterwards Mzilikazi was to meet another European, Robert Moffat, a missionary, and the two would become firm friends.

Back in uMgungundlovu, the Zulu royal kraal, Dingane's attention had now turned to Mzilikazi's Matabele. By May 1830 a Zulu army was en route to exterminate the man who Dingane considered to be a traitor. Five regiments were still absent in Mashona, and Mzilikazi, with no real allies to speak of, had to turn to his veterans. Mzilikazi cast around for allies and sent word to Sikhunyana, now chieftain of the Ndwandwe; he adamantly refused to help Mzilikazi.

The Matabele and Zulu met near the Mpebane and Bakane Rivers. For the first time like-armies were engaged, but the Zulu had a significant numerical advantage. Although the Zulu expeditionary force was led by Ndlela, the battle was actually conducted by Nzobo. Sheer weight of numbers settled the battle and the Matabele fell back in disorder. The Zulu pursued them until dusk, but with the absence of Ndlela, they paused and encamped for the night; this allowed the Matabele to escape. Mzilikazi adopted the same policy as Shaka had during the second Nwandwe invasion and had removed all of his non-combatants and razed his kraals to deny the Zulu any spoils of victory. Nonetheless, Ndlela succeeded in rounding up enough cattle to ensure that honour had been achieved in recompense for the cattle which Mzilikazi had denied Shaka. With that the Zulu army marched for home.

By the spring of 1831 the Matabele had sufficiently recovered to begin expansion once more. This time they headed towards the lands owned by Moshesh. Once again the Matabele faced a foe that was not prepared to meet them in open combat. Their stronghold, thab bosiu (the mountain at night) was a near impregnable mountaintop. The Matabele launched assaults on the position, but could make little progress. Moshesh's Basuto ultimately came to terms with the Matabele and offered cattle as a token of peace. Mzilikazi agreed peace terms and he could now turn his attention to the south.

A new coalition led by the Griqua and the Coranna and supported by elements of the Bataung and other Bechuna tribes, headed north and began raiding Matabele kraals. Once again the invaders were content with having appropriated thousands of cattle and began a march south once more. Again Mzilikazi had moved his troops overnight, waiting for an appropriate time to attack the unsuspecting raiders. As it turned out, Mzilikazi struck just before daybreak and managed to approach to within 200 metres before they were spotted. By nightfall the slaughter was complete and it is said that only three of the raiders managed to escape. The exact spot where the attack took place became known as Moordkop (Murder Hill).

Over the next year or more Mzilikazi invaded what is now Bechuanaland and incorporated it into his empire. These moves, amongst others, were bringing him into closer contact with white settlers. The beginning of 1834 saw Mzilikazi send Mkalipi, at the head of a Matabele army, to destroy what remained of the Barolong tribe on the north of the Molopo River. During this campaign Mkalipi was also charged with preventing strangers from crossing the Vaal River without Mzilikazi's permission. Mzilikazi had opened negotiations with the Cape government and in March 1836 a Matabele delegation, led by uMncumbata, signed a treaty with them. Under the terms of the treaty Mzilikazi was to protect any whites in his territory and not to initiate a war unless invaded.

Meanwhile, however, the Great Trek was in progress and the Boers were heading towards the Vaal River. Early in 1836 the immigrants, led by Louis Trickardt and Jan van Rensburg, crossed into Matabele territory. They did not encounter the Matabele and were probably wiped out by fever and smaller hostile tribes. During the same period another trekker party had reached the Vaal, this time led by Hendrik Potgieter. Almost at the same time, another Boer, Stephanus Erasmus, had crossed into Mzilikazi's territory whilst on a hunting trip. It was Erasmus's men that first encountered the Matabele; one morning they found themselves surrounded by 600 warriors. The Boers fled for the only protection available to them; the trekker families with Potgieter. The result was inevitable and several Boers were killed and a large number of their cattle appropriated. Now that the Matabele knew that the Boers had illegally crossed the Vaal, they could only expect the worst and consequently the trekker families were rounded up and they formed a laager around a hill which was to become known as Vegkop (battle hill).

On 15 October 1836, 6,000 Matabele, led by Mkalipi, headed for Potgieter's laager. A twenty-man, mounted Boer force rode out to attack. Potgieter's mounted patrol fought a retiring engagement back to the laager. The Matabele surrounded the Boers and in the space of an hour or so the battle was decided, with the Matabele making at least two futile attacks on the laager. Several hundred warriors were alleged to have been killed, but nonetheless Mkalipi retreated, taking with him around 100 horses, 500 cattle and as many as 50,000 sheep. Amongst the Boers in Potgieter's laager was the future President of South Africa, Paul Kruger.

On 25 October messengers arrived at eGabeni, where Mzilikazi awaited news. Mzilikazi believed that the Boers had been routed given the fact that the regiments were returning such a large haul of livestock. Potgieter, meanwhile had dispatched his brother, Hermanus, to Thaba Nchu to the south, where he encountered another group of immigrants, led by Gerrit Maritz. Teams of oxen were provided by James Archbell and Moroko, the chief of the Barolong tribe. These were necessary because Potgieter's wagons were stranded at Vegkop. The Boers were adamant that their trek should not be stopped by the Matabele and that Mzilikazi's armies would have to be shattered before any further attempts to cross the Vaal were made. In the last two months of 1836 the Boer immigrants conferred with Peter David, a Griqua captain, to launch an expedition against the Matabele. Consequently, on 2 January 1837, Potgieter, Maritz, David, Sikonyela (son of Mantatisi) and Matlab (a Barolong chief) headed into the Matabele kingdom, accompanied by just over 100 mounted Boers. Their first target was the Mosega region which contained Mkalipi's stronghold at Mkwahla. The invading force attacked Mkalipi's main kraal and despite being heavily outnumbered by the Matabele, who launched several assaults on the Boers, they were successful in scattering Mkalipi's men.

It had taken the Boers some two weeks to reach this area and just one morning to scatter the Matabele. After the rout at Mkwahla, the Matabele made one last stand, but were scattered by twenty-one Boers led by a man called Steyn. The invasion had been a complete success so far, but Potgieter and Maritz decided that their horses were too exhausted and in too poor a condition to press on. They therefore returned to the Mosega Valley, rounded up some 7,000 head of cattle, burned all the kraals and headed home.

The news of the Matabele defeat soon reached the ears of Dingane and in May 1837 a large Zulu force crossed the Pongolo River and headed towards the outlying area of Mzilikazi's kingdom. They were soon detected and a battle took place near the Marico River. At first the Zulu had the upper hand and at least one of Mzilikazi's regiments (the iziMpangele) was slaughtered. The Zulu seized thousands of Matabele cattle, but a counter-attack managed to inflict heavy casualties on the Zulu and most of the cattle were retrieved. The Zulu army did not return home to emGungundlovu until later in the year, where it claimed it had decisively defeated the Matabele. In truth neither side had won a decisive victory; this was the last time that the Matabele and Zulu would meet on a battlefield.

Meanwhile, the Boers had founded Winburg on the Bet River. Potgieter and Maritz bickered about leadership and the next most appropriate step for them to take. They had been joined by Pieter Uys and together with Potgieter he led a commando of 360 men across the Vaal in October 1837. They reached the Mosega Valley on 2 November and found the whole area still in desolation. They next moved on Tshwenyane, Marapu's military kraal. They approached the kraal shortly before sunrise and surrounded it. Marapu was not present as he was at eGabeni with Mzilikazi. Once again the Boers slaughtered the Matabele, despite several brave charges. The Boers torched Tshwenyane and proceeded to hunt down the fleeing warriors, razing every kraal they encountered. The pursuit and destruction continued for the next two days; the Boers then headed south-west to deal with a large Matabele garrison, commanded by Kampu. Unbeknown to them, Mzilikazi had sent a considerable force to reinforce Kampu under Marapu.

The Boers, advancing in a long line, with two groups to protect their flanks, advanced on the Matabele army. The Matabele assumed the chest and horns formation and charged to close with the Boers. On the flanks the Boer horsemen prevented the tips of the horns from encircling them, whilst the main body of Boers concentrated on the chest. The firepower buckled the Matabele lines and soon Mzilikazi's army was in flight, with the Boers relentlessly pursuing them. The Boers stopped their pursuit and concentrated on burning Kampu's kraal, allowing the Matabele to reform. Once again they attempted to encircle the Boer horsemen, only to fail again. This time the Boers hunted the Matabele until dusk, by which time their horses were exhausted. Mzilikazi and what remained of the Matabele army flooded into eGabeni. It was only a matter of time before the Boers would attack eGabeni, which was Mzilikazi's last stronghold.

The attack took place on the morning of 9 November. The Matabele could muster some 12,000 warriors; they would be led by Mzilikazi, Mkalipi, Marapu, Kampu and Sibekhu. Mzilikazi decided to adopt a tactic which had been used against him in the past, almost to a disastrous effect. He had herded his cattle ahead of his army and proposed to drive them at the Boers. As the Boers advanced the cattle were stampeded, but Boer musket fire managed to drive the cattle back towards the Matabele. This succeeded in breaking up the cohesion of the regiments and before the Boers even closed, the bulk of the army was retreating. The Boers relentlessly pursued the Matabele until 12 November, by which time the defeated Matabele had traversed the passes of the Dwarsberg range. The Boers retreated back to Kampu's military kraal, with thousands of head of cattle. They renamed the hill Maaierskop (maggot hill) on account of the hundreds of rotting corpses which lay there. Although the Boers had decisively defeated the Matabele, seized their lands and stolen their cattle, Mzilikazi was still alive.

On the other side of the Dwarsberg, the Matabele had split into two groups. Gudwane Ndeweni, at the head of the Amnyama-Makanda (blackheads division) led the bulk of the women and children towards the Limpopo River. He cut a swathe through the tribes in the region and settled in what would become Southern Rhodesia at a place called Gibixhegu.

Meanwhile Mzilikazi had headed into Bechuanaland in an area known as Shoshong where he was attacked by Seghoma's Bamangwato. He believed that the Matabele's strength had been broken, but Mzilikazi defeated him, burned his kraals and appropriated his cattle. Mzilikazi continued his march through a desolate landscape, heading for Lake Ngami. As he approached the Okavango swamps he was attacked by the Makololo tribe. The engagements were indecisive and Mzilikazi headed south.

Meanwhile back at Gibixhegu, Gudwane feared that Mzilikazi was dead and that the rest of the Matabele had been slaughtered. They therefore decided to discuss the prospect of appointing a successor. Some favoured Kulumane, the heir apparent, but Gudwane sent patrols out to discover what had become of Mzilikazi. By the beginning of 1840 Mzilikazi was in northern Bechuanaland, in the Makarikari salt pans region and it was here they encountered one of Gudwane's patrols. Mzilikazi could now make his way to the rest of his tribe, but he wasted little time in accusing Gudwane and several other indunas of treason. Gudwane and the other indunas were executed and Kulumane was strangled, along with another son, Ubuhlelo. An infant, Lobengula, another son, was smuggled into hiding and later became Mzilikazi's favourite and his heir.

Mzilikazi established his royal kraal at Mahlokohloko (Ntabazinduna – the hill of the indunas), where Gudwane and the others had been executed. Gibixhego was abandoned and the whole area was subdivided into districts. Over the next five years Mzilikazi would concentrate on subjugating the local tribes, including the Barozwi and the Makalanga. The next tribe to be invaded by the Matabele was the Mashona, but Mzilikazi would suffer a serious reversal at the hands of the Makololo.

Mzilikazi sent 2,000 warriors in search of Sebitoane's Makololo, encountering them on the banks of the Zambesi River. The Matabele made a deal with a river tribe, the Batonka, to transport the army to an island in the middle of the river. From here the river tribe would then convey the army across the Zambesi. The Matabele were to be double-crossed and only half of the army was conveyed to the island and abandoned there. By the time the Makololo landed on the island they were too weak to resist. The much weakened remnants of the Matabele army made their way back to Maholokohloko, but only eight made it home. Of the eight, three were regimental commanders who were sentenced to death for their failure.

In their new territory the Matabele flourished. It became known as Matabeleland. Kraals, military barracks, cattle posts and extensive agriculture were established. The Boers had not forgotten the Matabele, however, and Potgieter still smarted from the loss of the cattle and the flocks. They had learned that the Matabele had settled to the north of the Limpopo River. By 1847 Potgieter had pinpointed exactly where the Matabele now were and he resolved to retrieve what Mzilikazi owed him.

The Boer force was opposed by the Zwangendaba regiment, led by Mbigo. The Boers had already begun raiding the Matabele cattle posts and were sending the stolen cattle back towards the Shashi River. The Boers had contracted some Bapedi herdsmen to take the cattle back and Mbigo's men managed to ambush them, slaughter the herdsmen and retrieve the cattle. In retribution, Potgieter made for the royal kraal at Mahlokohloko, but found it deserted and had to content himself with looting it and then burning it down. The Boers then retired from Matabeleland.

There was, however, to be a change in relations between Mzilikazi and the Boers and in 1852 Potgieter sent representatives to seek a peace treaty with the Matabele. Further discussions took place in December 1852 at Zoutpansberg, a settlement which Potgieter had recently founded. As part of the treaty Mzilikazi agreed not to allow firearms and ammunition to be trafficked in Matabeleland and that they would arrest any traders or hunters smuggling weapons. Mzilikazi also agreed to provide auxiliary troops if the Boer republic was ever invaded. The treaty was signed in January 1853 and just a month later Potgieter died.

By 1854 Mzilikazi was exhausted and was suffering from ill health which would ultimately lead to his death several years later. He had become morose, short-tempered and somewhat unpredictable and his senior advisors believed that he was bewitched. In 1860 a lung sickness epidemic broke out amongst the royal herds; it would claim three-quarters of the Matabele herd. In 1862 the loss of the herds was compounded by a terrible drought which wiped out the harvest. Mzilikazi arranged military expeditions to raid outlying areas to secure food for his people. He sent three columns; the first to Mashonaland, the second to the area around Lake Ngami and the third into Seghoma's Bamangwato territory in northern Bechuanaland. The raids were generally successful; the Bamangwato provided much-needed cattle and grain. Mzilikazi was also forced to launch an expedition against one of his own sub-chieftains, Makhobi, to the south of his kingdom, after he had refused to accompany the Matabele armies in their attacks on the Bamangwato.

One of Mzilikazi's most pressing problems was keeping white traders out of areas in which the Matabele had traditionally raided. He feared that they would supply his enemies with firearms. By 1865 there were considerable numbers of Europeans seeking access to Matabeleland. Some were hunters, others less scrupulous individuals who would trade with anyone, for anything for profit. On one occasion in 1865 a hunting party shot over 200 elephants in Mashonaland, netting them over five tons of ivory. The leader of the party, Jan Viljoen, made the mistake of selling five guns to one of Mzilikazi's vassals. Mzilikazi was furious and would neither trust Viljoen or, to a lesser extent, other Boers again.

The autumn of 1866 saw an even greater influx of Europeans in Matabeleland. Mzilikazi was by now very ill and was grateful to any European that offered him medicines to sustain him. He frequently hallucinated that Shaka was at the head of a vast Zulu army, marching towards them to wipe them out. He even sent scouts south, but they all returned to tell him that there was no threat.

Unfortunately it would not be the Zulu that would bring about the downfall of the Matabele, it was gold. In July 1867 Karl Mauch discovered a vast deposit on a tributary of the Umfuli River. He hastened to Pretoria and within months gold-miners from as far afield as California and Australia were on their way to South Africa. In early 1868 a Boer delegation, led by Jan Viljoen arrived to negotiate with Mzilikazi to buy the Tati area, which contained the new goldfields. Mzilikazi was told that if he sold the area to the Boer then they would prevent other Europeans from entering Matabeleland. Mzilikazi refused, but his health was fading fast and he finally lost his battle with old age and ill health on 5 September.

The body lay in state for fifty-six days until it was interred at enTumbane (little hill) in a cave in part of the Matopo Range. Mzilikazi's death precipitated a period of enormous confusion. Some believed that Kulumane was still alive and in exile. Ultimately the only true heir, Lobengula was proposed, but he feared that if he accepted the offer he would be assassinated by several other factions who had alternate successors in mind. A man did emerge who claimed to be Kulumane. He was a groom of the Secretary of Native Affairs in Natal, Theophilus Shepstone. The man, living under the name of uKhanda, attempted to persuade the Bamangwato tribe to invade Matabeleland to press his claim. He failed to persuade the Bamangwato and faded back into obscurity.

Ultimately Lobengula was crowned on 17 March 1870. He built a new royal kraal at Gibixhegu (later Bulawayo). Nonetheless, Mbigo and his Zwangendaba regiment refused to recognize Lobengula. The new king mustered his regiments and sent them north to where Mbigo's military kraal lay. After a fifty-mile march and two assaults on the kraal they overwhelmed Mbigo and the Zwangendaba and a brief civil war was over.

Enormous numbers of Europeans established goldfields in the Tati region. Exclusive mining rights were granted to them by uMncumbata, who had served as a regent of the tribe after Mzilikazi's death, had supervised the murder of Kulumane and had personally nominated Logengula as Mzilikazi's successor. Over the next eighteen years the Europeans established themselves firmly around the goldfields. From the very beginning there were clashes between Matabele warriors and encroaching settlers. But matters came to a head in 1893 when war broke out.

In October 1893, in response to a series of attacks by the Matabele, Major Forbes and Major Wilson, at the head of units of the Chartered Company, marched on Bulawayo. Towards the end of October they encountered a Matabele army near the Shangani River. The Matabele were beaten but not decisively and retreated in good order. Another Matabele attack took place at the beginning of November, as Forbes and Wilson approached the Bembisi River. The white troops, armed with machine guns, apparently all but wiped out the Imbezu and the Ingubo regiments. After this disastrous engagement Lobengula abandoned Bulawayo and headed north towards the Zambesi River. Forbes and Wilson, with nothing to be gained by continuing to march on Bulawayo, fell back to the Shangani River. On 3 December, with Major Wilson at the head of a cavalry patrol, the invaders attempted to locate Lobengula. They found the king near the River Shangani, but when Wilson and his troops approached they were ambushed and massacred.

Meanwhile, the bulk of the Matabele army was being decimated by troops from the British South Africa Company and the Bechuanaland border police, supported by his existing units. Lobengula had no option but to seek a peace treaty, but before this could be signed he died of a fever in January 1894.

The land, formerly known as Matabeleland, covering the area between the Limpopo and the Zambesi Rivers, now became Southern Rhodesia. The kingdom forged by the resourceful Mzilikazi was no more.

Chapter Five

Dingane kaSenzangakhona

At some point in mid-1824 a determined attempt was made to murder Shaka. He had been stabbed through his left arm and the blade had penetrated his rib cage. The attempted assassination was immediately linked with Zwide and two Zulu regiments were dispatched to find the assassins and exact punishment on the Ndwandwe. Three men were indeed captured and killed and their bodies brought back to kwaBulawayo. The regiments went on into Ndwandwe territory, burned a number of kraals and brought back over 800 cattle. The chaos and grieving demanded by Shaka was witnessed by Henry Frances Fynn, of the Fairwell Trading Company, who had visited Shaka to gain a title to Port Natal and around 3,500 square miles of territory.

Shaka waited until July or August 1826 before he decided to deal with the Ndwandwe once and for all. One of Zwide's surviving sons, Sikhunyana, had managed to organize a new army and upwards of 40,000 Zulu warriors were mustered to deal with them. The Zulu army marched to a mountainous area near the Intombi River, where the Ndwandwe had established a defensive position. The Ndwandwe occupied the summit of a rocky hill with their non-combatants safely protected behind them. The Zulu army approached to within around 20 metres and then charged. In the next hour and a half the Ndwandwe tribe virtually ceased to exist, as men, women and children were slaughtered and 60,000 cattle taken. Fynn, who witnessed the battle, estimated that 40,000 Ndwandwe were killed. Sikhunyana managed to escape and despite Zulu regiments being sent off to find him, he was never found.

In 1827 Shaka sent a third army to find and destroy Mzilikazi's Kumalo. The 5,000 men were accompanied by Nathaniel Isaacs, a colleague of Fynn, and ten musket-armed men. The muskets appeared to be the deciding factor and the Kumalo surrendered their cattle and goats and as far as the Zulu were concerned honour had been achieved.

Perhaps the turning point as far as Shaka was concerned was the death of his mother, Nandi. His grief was unbounded. He ordered that no crops should be planted for a year, that no one should drink milk, and that pregnant women were to be killed along with their husbands. In short, a reign of terror overtook the Zulu and, above all, Shaka required all of his subjects to be as genuinely distraught as him. The mourning lasted for at least three months and by the beginning of 1828 Shaka was considering his next military campaign.

Shaka launched a raid on the amaMpondo, led by Faku; he would then attack the Tembus. His base of operations was a new kraal on the Umzimkulu River. Shaka divided his army into two divisions; Mdlaka would deal with Faku and a second division, under Manyundela, would deal with the Tembus. Faku proved no match for the Zulu and his tribe scattered. Meanwhile the second division beat the Tembus in battle, during which Manyundela was killed and 10,000 cattle were captured.

The campaign had sent shock waves through the Cape colony and Major Dundas, at the head of some Imperial troops and Boers, attacked a native force on 20 July, believing them to be Zulu. They were, in fact, the emaNgwaneni tribe under Matiwane. The unfortunate Matiwane blundered into a second Cape colony force of around 1,000 mounted cavalry and Boers and up to 18,000 Tembu allies under Lieutenant Colonel Somerset. The engagement took place on 26 August and the emaNgwaneni were virtually wiped out. No sooner had this campaign been completed than Shaka dispatched his army to deal with tribes in the north-east.

The conspiracy to kill Shaka was probably led initially by Senzangakhona's sister, Mkabayi, who believed that Shaka had poisoned Nandi. She had approached Dingane and Mhlangana who had agreed that Shaka should be killed. They enlisted the support of Mbopa, who as an Induna organized Shaka's domestic arrangements. Both Dingane and Mhlangana were to accompany the army on its expedition to the north-east, but they pretended to be too ill to go into combat. Shaka was unaware of any of this.

On 22 September 1828 the amaMpondo arrived with gifts for the king. Mbopa had hidden an assegai under his cloak and Dingane and Mhlangana concealed themselves nearby. As the amaMpondo delegation presented itself, Mbopa berated them for being late. Shaka joined in and at that point Dingane and Mhlangana rushed Shaka and repeatedly stabbed him with their spears. His body was eventually tumbled into a grain pit.

To a large extent any successor would need the full support of the army. The army was still engaged under Mdlaka against the renegade Ndwandwe Soshangane. Mdlaka had wiped out the emaNtshalini for failing to observe Nandi's death in a suitable manner. He had then struck out to deal with Soshangane somewhere to the north-east of Delagoa Bay. Soshangane had taken up a strong position and was all but besieged by Mdlaka's army, but Soshangane had led a dawn attack against the Zulu flank and had temporarily spread panic, despite the fact that he was outnumbered ten to one. By the time Mdlaka rallied his troops Soshangane had disappeared and he decided to give up the pursuit.

Meanwhile, Mbopa had been acting as regent and Dingane and Mhlangana had established their own kraals near kwaDukuja. Before the army arrived, Mbopa, at the head of the recently formed Nyosi regiment, moved against Shaka's brother (by Nandi), Ngwadi. It might be remembered that Ngwadi had dealt with Senzangakhona's heir and by killing him had made the path clear for Shaka to inherit the crown of the Zulu. By all accounts it was a swift and brutal dawn attack on Ngwadi's kraal. This act alone meant that the assassins now had nothing to fear from any of Nandi's sons. Relations between Dingane and Mhlangana had deteriorated and, after Mhlangana had attempted to murder Dingane in October, Dingane had him killed. Shortly afterwards the army, or at least what remained of it, arrived back with

Mdlaka. Only Mdlaka stood in Dingane's way, but he too was killed. Foolishly as it would transpire, Dingane allowed his own younger brother, Mpande to survive during this cull.

Dingane, at around thirty years old, had fought in the majority of Shaka's campaigns over the past twelve years, with the amaWombe regiment. The death of Shaka had unravelled many of the ties which had controlled some of the more independent tribes. The first challenge came from Nqetho, chieftain of the Kwabe. He demanded the return of one of the tribe's women who had been held captive in Shaka's kraal. Dingane refused and Nqetho panicked and headed south with his tribe and cattle. He desperately tried to gain support from other clans but when they refused he attacked them and took their cattle. Dingane sent an army to deal with Nqetho but they were content to seize a number of his cattle and return to their king. Nqetho re-established his tribe near the Umzimvubo River, neighbouring Faku's Mpondo.

Dingane set about reorganizing Shaka's regiments and to create new ones of his own. He established his own kraal in mid-1829 to the south-east of Shaka's royal kraal and named it uMgungundlovu, appointing Nongalaza kaNondela as commander of the army. At some point in late 1829 Matiwane and his clan, the amaNgwane, who had fled during Shaka's reign, returned, having been roughly handled by Somerset. Dingane welcomed him at first and allowed what remained of the tribe to settle close to his new royal kraal. However, shortly after this welcome Dingane had the whole clan slaughtered, with Matiwane being lavishly executed on a hill which became known as kwaMatiwane Hill.

Although Dingane would send his armies against the Swazi under Sobhuza, the campaigns were unproductive, as was the campaign in 1832 against Mzilizaki's Matabele. A three month expedition against the Matabele culminated in a single battle which ended in stalemate. Dingane also attacked the white settlers and the Zulu dissidents they were harbouring in Delagoa Bay. Two attacks were made in July 1833 and again on 17 September. The settlement was stormed but the Zulu were only hunting for a Portuguese slaver, Dionisio Antonio Ribeiro, who had seized some Zulu during slaving expeditions between 1825 and 1831.

Although Ribeiro initially escaped he was later captured by the Zulu and executed.

Dingane launched another campaign against the Swazi in 1836. Much of the army had not seen active service for around three years and some thirty settlers, led by John Cane, accompanied the Zulu army. Once again there was no decisive battle, but the Zulu returned to Dingane leading thousands of captured cattle.

In January 1837 Mzilikazi had been decisively defeated at the hands of the Boers. Dingane was elated with what had befallen Mzilikazi and he determined to take advantage of the situation. Dingane dispatched an army to deal with Mzilikazi once and for all, but the battle was indecisive and the army returned to Dingane in the September, again simply driving vast herds of captured cattle.

The Great Trek had begun in 1834 and from October 1836 to mid-1837 had relentlessly attacked the Matabele and seized thousands of their cattle. The Boers now stood at the edge of Dingane's kingdom. Piet Retief requested permission from the Zulu king to settle on the edge of his territory. He conferred with Dingane, who accused him of having stolen 300 of his royal cattle. Dingane promised that Retief could have the land if he could prove his innocence. Unbeknown to Retief, who was bound for Durban, Dingane had ordered the chieftain Sigwebana to murder him en route. The chieftain refused to cooperate and Retief managed to get to Durban. In a rage Dingane scattered and slaughtered most of Sigwebana's clan.

Meanwhile, in eager anticipation of a settlement, over 1,000 Boer wagons had formed up around the Thukela (Tugela) River. Dingane naturally assumed that this premature move was nothing more than the beginnings of an invasion. Retief, meanwhile, rode into Sikonyela's baTlokwa territory, which bordered the Zulu kingdom. He kidnapped the chieftain and ransomed him for 700 cattle. Retief sold 400 of the cattle and began driving the remaining 300 towards uMgungundhlovu (the cattle had been rustled by Sikonyela from the Zulu). Retief was accompanied by nearly seventy Boers and a number of black servants. He paraded the cattle and his men outside the kraal and told Dingane how he had come by the cattle, horses and guns taken from the baTlokwa.

Dingane demanded the horses and guns but Retief refused to hand them over.

On 4 February 1838 Dingane ceded Natal (from the Umzimvubu River to the Thukela River, including Durban) to Retief. Retief was elated and two days later the Boers were invited to a farewell celebration. Dingane had called his regiments to his kraal and at the king's signal all of the Boers were seized, dragged off to a hill and impaled. Retief was the last to die.

Dingane sent a message to the settlers in Delagoa Bay that they should not be alarmed, but had simultaneously sent three regiments to deal with the Boers who were gathering to enter the Zulu kingdom. Just before dawn the regiments swept across the laagers, slaughtering nearly 300 settlers and 250 servants. The regiments returned to Dingane with 10,000 captured cattle and the die had been well and truly cast.

The remaining Boers were now led by Gerrit Maritz, Piet Uys and Hendrik Potgieter who determined to launch an offensive against Dingane. Before the Boers could muster, John Cane, with a handful of Europeans and some 2,000 tribesmen from the iziNkumbi, launched an assault in March, capturing some 4,000 cattle. Meanwhile, Uys and Potgieter crossed the Buffalo River in early April, bent on revenge.

Battle focus

Italeni (near uMgungundlovu,
5 kilometres south-west of Dingaanstat)

9 or 11 April 1838

The Voortrekker commando had left the Blaauwkrans River during 5–6 April; the two columns amounted to a little under 350 men. They crossed the Thukela River (at present day Helpmekaar), passed the site of the future battlefield of Isandlwana and encountered a Zulu force, possibly on 9 April.

The Voortrekkers captured a number of Zulu stragglers who told them that Dingane's main force was mustered at his Royal kraal (uMgungundlovu). In order to approach the kraal, the Voortrekkers would have to pass through the Sebonen Nek, barely half-an-hour's ride from uMgungundlovu. Unbeknown to the Voortrekkers, Dingane had set a trap here, a trap they were about to ride straight into and where they would face 7–8,000 Zulu.

Led by Piet Uys, the emigrant farmers waited around 6 kilometres from uMgungundlovu. They could see the mountain pass was clear, but at the end were two hills covering the pass. On each of the hills were Zulu regiments and a third impi was just in sight in the valley beyond.

The Voortrekker opted to attack the impi on the right-hand side. Some forty men were detached to guard the supply horses and the bulk of the commando rode forward to engage the Zulu. The Voortrekkers dismounted at around 40 metres from the leading Zulu regiment. The volleys appeared to shatter the first Zulu regiment and the one stationed behind it; the third and remaining regiment broke and fled.

It appeared that the battle had been easily won; the Voortrekkers now made an attempt to clear the left hill, this time firing from the saddle. Unlike the right-sided hill, the Zulu immediately charged the Voortrekkers (only around twenty had approached to within musket range). The Voortrekkers broke and fled, taking with them the bulk of the mounted men. Piet Uys' contingent was now isolated and the Zulu had all but surrounded them. Uys sent a messenger requesting Potgieter (at the head of the retiring Voortrekkers) to cover him, stating that they should press on. Potgieter and his commando were unimpressed and refused to assist.

The Malan brothers, with Uys, began pursuing Zulu stragglers into a gorge. It was clear to Uys that the Zulu were attempting to lure the men away in order to surround and kill them.

Uys led around fifteen volunteers to extract the brothers, reaching them almost as the Zulu horns had closed around them. In the running fight, Uys was the first to be mortally wounded. One of the Malan brothers' horses was now killed, but he climbed up behind his brother. Another Voortrekker, Jan Meyer, lost his horse but the heavily bleeding Uys carried him to safety. In the next series of retreats the Malan brothers were cut off and killed. Pieter Nel was next to fall as the Zulu closed in on the terrified and exhausted Voortrekkers. As the Voortrekkers reached a hill they split to go around it left and right. Gert and Louis Nel, together with the Malan brothers' father, Dawid, were trapped and overwhelmed.

One of the last to fall was Dirkie Uys, Piet Uys' son. There are two accounts of his death. Either he was pulled from his horse and killed on the spot as his mount floundered crossing the stream, or he was actually captured by the Zulu. If the latter is the case, it is said that he was killed on Dingane's instruction and a broth was made from his flesh to doctor the regiments. In either event, his body was never recovered from the battlefield. If he did die on the battlefield, it was either as he crossed the stream or beside the dying form of his father near the stream where exhaustion and loss of blood had forced the older Uys to be abandoned.

Meanwhile, Potgieter and the bulk of the commando were trapped atop a hill. They held for an hour and a half against increasing Zulu pressure and attacks. Ultimately, the Voortrekkers concentrated their fire to sweep a path, through which they could escape the ring of Zulu around them. The bulk of the Voortrekkers did indeed escape, but they were forced to abandon their pack horses and ammunition.

The battle had, so far, raged across no less than 24 kilometres of rough ground. It was not yet over. The Zulu now lay in wait for Potgieter at the Umhlatuzi River, but the Voortrekkers managed to shoot their way through the Zulu screen.

Ultimately, the Voortrekkers returned to their laager on 12 April. They were dubbed the Vlugkommando (flight) and hard lessons had been learned about fighting the Zulu in the open. The Boers would not make the same mistake quite so easily again.

Some time after the battle at Ncome River in December 1838 the Wenkommando returned to the area of the running battle of Italeni to collect the bones of the Voortrekker dead. Piet Uys' body was identified by six silver buttons which had been attached to a waistcoat, as well as the obvious remains of an old skull fracture he had sustained many years before.

Cane, operating from Port Natal, now launched a second attack on the Zulu. Calling themselves the Grand Army of Natal, they were commanded by Robert Biggar, John Cane and John Stubbs. They were unaware that Uys had been defeated and left Port Natal on 14 April 1838, reaching the Thukela River on 16 April.

Battle focus

Thukela (Tugela)

17 April 1838

The Grand Army of Natal was nominally commanded by Robert Biggar (whose father had been a solider), John Cane (a carpenter, experienced hunter and had commanded his own men in skirmishes in the past) and John Stubbs (a trader).

The Grand Army's strength amounted to eighteen settlers supported by some 400 auxiliaries from their own hunting retinues. The settlers were heavily armed and the auxiliaries proficient in the use of the musket. This semi-experienced core was supported by up to 3,000 men drawn from the refugees living around Port Natal. They were traditionally armed, but dubious in terms of experience, temperament

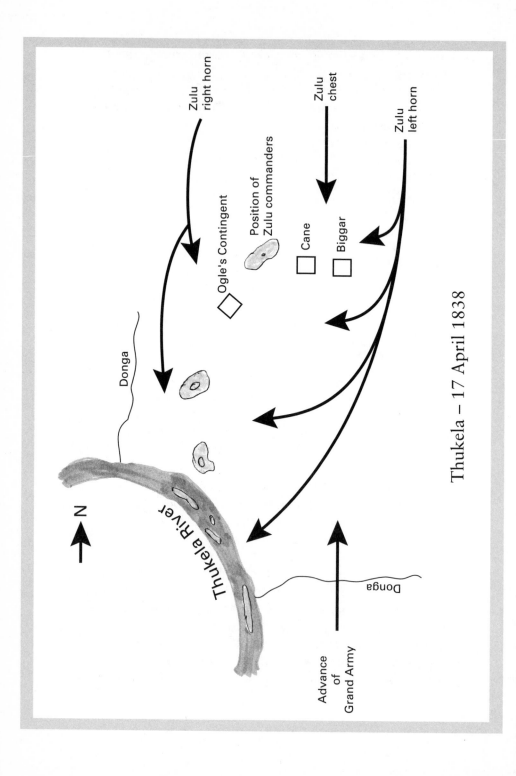

Thukela – 17 April 1838

and enthusiasm. It seems possible that the men had white calico tied around their heads to mark them as members of the Grand Army.

It is unclear whether the Grand Army was aware of the death and defeat of Piet Uys, but in any event it seems clear that the Zulu was expecting an invasion from this quarter.

The Grand Army reached the banks of the River Thukela towards the close of light on 16 April. They proposed a crossing at the Lower Drift, with the scouting force of musket-armed auxiliaries crossing under the command of a Luthuli chieftain called Funwayo kaMpopoma. The nearest Zulu homestead was deserted, which should have alerted the invaders to the fact that the Zulu were aware of the incursion. Two Zulu scouts were captured here, roughed up during interrogation, then shot.

Funwayo kaMpopoma and his men slipped back across the river to report. The choice was stark; either to seize the initiative to cross before the Zulu army arrived, or to wait on this side of the river until the Zulu showed their hand. Cane was all for sitting it out in the relative safety of their position, but Biggar wanted to cross and close with the Zulu on his terms. A compromise of sorts was reached; the Grand Army would cross before first light in the morning. Their immediate first objective was the Zulu homestead of iNdondakusuka.

Dingane was perfectly aware of the vulnerability of this area to attack. He had established a number of Royal kraals in the region. Nominally, this part of the kingdom was ruled by his brother (and future successor), Mpande kaSenzangakhona. Militarily, the troops in the region were commanded by Nongalaza kaNondela, an astute Zulu induna. The area was known as Hlomendlini, with the white (senior) Mhlope troops and the black (more junior) Mnyama regiments. As ominously for the Grand Army, their target, iNdondakusuka, was the home of Zulu kaNogandaya, a close friend of Shaka, who had fought valiantly for the Zulu during the Ndwandwe campaigns. Zulu kaNogandaya commanded the uMwanqa regiment and had fought against the whites before (he had led the expedition that had destroyed John Cane's homestead in 1831).

As planned, the Grand Army crossed the Thukela shortly before dawn and headed for iNdondakusuka, which was little more than two miles into Zululand. As the sun rose, the Grand Army was in position and their musketeers delivered a devastating volley into the kraal.

The Zulu non-combatants had been evacuated and the kraal simply concealed Zulu scouts. Some were cut down by the volleys. One wounded Zulu was captured and he confidently told the settlers before he died that the Zulu army was close by and would soon crush them. Indeed the Zulu army, probably commanded by Nongalaza kaNondela leading the Hlomendlini Mhlope and Zulu kaNogandaya commanding the Hlomendlini Mnyana, were closing fast. They had almost certainly spent the night in the Eshowe area. The musketry from the Grand Army hastened the Zulu movement; they surged through the depressions and rough ground, adopting the traditional bull's head formation (izimpondo zankomo).

As the Zulu deployed, it was the chest that felt the force of the settlers' gunfire first. Facing them was a British deserter, Robert Joyce (formerly of the 72nd) commanding a group of settlers and auxiliaries. The fire was falling so that the chest was stopped; it then retired into cover. With the Zulu attacks stalled, the Grand Army could now confidently predict that the next assault would come from the horns.

In anticipation of this, Cane and Biggar stationed themselves to deal with the Zulu left horn and Henry Ogle's contingent to cover the ground through which the Zulu right horn was expected. Both horns were driven back by the firepower, but Ogle's men, figuring that following up the Zulu retreat would leave them exposed and cut off from the rest of the army, retired. (It is important to note that Henry Ogle did not take part in the invasion, but had given permission to his retainers to take part).

Nongalaza kaNondela spotted the retrograde move and ordered the right wing to renew their attacks. This time, with Ogle's men falling back, the Zulu managed to get into hand-to-hand combat. The outcome was never in doubt and the invaders were slaughtered whilst others desperately tried to reach the river. The Zulu cut them off from the only safe crossing and several had to jump off the cliffs into the river to escape.

The Grand Army's left was gone; Nongalaza kaNondela ordered renewed attacks from his chest and left wing regiments. The troops under Biggar and Cane held their ground, inflicting heavy casualties on the Zulu. Wary of being surrounded and cut off from the river, the Grand Army began to retreat. Little by little, the Zulu were closing in; Biggar fell when a Zulu regiment managed to charge home on the right of the settler's line. Cane was hit by two spears and slumped off his horse to his doom. Stubbs, too, fell as the Grand Army was shattered by the surging Zulu regiments.

At this stage the Grand Army was almost surrounded; the auxiliaries tore off their calico headbands and were either shot by their own side or identified by the Zulu and speared. It was now a question of every man for himself. Few made it to the river; many who did were drowned.

Zulu casualties can be estimated at around 2,000, although this may be an exaggeration. As for the Grand Army; four white survived of the eighteen, very few of the mixed race musketeers and over half of the auxiliaries were slaughtered.

The defeat of the British settlers at Thukela effectively put them out of the war. Dingane was winning the struggle against the encroachment from the Europeans, yet the Boers had not given up. Ten thousand Zulu, under Ndlela kaOmpisi, had been dispatched to deal with the Boer encroachment and on 13 August the Zulu army closed to attack.

Battle focus

emGabeni (Veglaer – or fight laager)

13–15 August 1838

The Boers were commanded by J. Potgieter and Hans dons de Lange, numbering some seventy-five men. They had formed a laager on a ridge (known as Gatsrand) in the Bushman's River valley. Around 290 wagons had been formed up in a double line in the shape of a triangle which ran parallel to the river. Pits had been dug on the approaches to the laager. The women and children were provided with plank and hide shelters within the laager.

The Zulu army was spotted by herd boys at around 10.00. Once the Zulu had realized they had been spotted, they deployed out of column and into the bull's head formation. The right horn swung around, as did the left, to encircle the laager. The assaults began on the Boer position at around 12.00. The Boer fire cut into the charging Zulu assisted by a single cannon firing canister. Some Zulu managed to make it to the laager, but the hides and planking prevented them from getting inside. The Zulu temporarily retreated and the Boers launched a series of mounted counter-attacks to drive them back. Ultimately the Zulu retreated out of range and seemed to be content to spend the night slaughtering and eating the Boer cattle.

The following morning saw the Boers attempt to lure the Zulu into attacking the laager again, but this time the Zulu tried to set fire to the laager with no great success. Several attacks were launched but again these met with failure. With some of the Zulu rounding up the Boer cattle, the bulk of the Zulu army retreated, setting fire to grass to cover their retreat.

The Zulu were still in the vicinity on 15 August but seemed ill-disposed to attack. The Boers, likewise, were exhausted and hungry and chose not to provoke another attack.

Reluctantly Ndlela retreated with the Boer cattle to report to Dingane.

Although the Zulu had failed to overwhelm the laager, they had seized the Boer cattle and for that alone the engagement was a draw.

As far as the Boers were concerned, facing the Zulu on open ground was near suicidal, as had been proven at Italeni and Thukela. The Boers were heartened by the fact that an overwhelming Zulu force had failed to overrun a laager with relatively little firepower. Pretorius, therefore, determined to repeat this successful technique and take the war into Dingane's territory.

Battle focus

Ncome (Blood) River

December 16 1838

The Boer Voortrekkers, commanded by Andries Pretorius, took up a defensive position on the left (western) bank of the River Ncome. It was a formidable position, protected by the steep left bank and further protected by a donga. Pretorius could call upon some 472 men, plus 200 grooms of mixed race and 130 wagoners. The primary defensive position, a laager, consisted of some sixty-four wagons. He had been joined by Alexander Biggar and 120 of his followers, bent on revenge for the death of Biggar's sons.

The Voortrekkers were perfectly aware of the presence of a large Zulu army, possibly between 12,000 and 16,000. The river was fordable at two points in this area; if the Zulu attacked they could only approach the laager via these two drifts. The circular laager was all but impregnable within the defensive position, however it also housed the 1,500 or so oxen and horses.

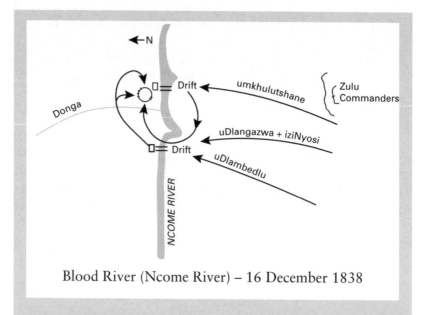

Blood River (Ncome River) – 16 December 1838

The Zulu army was commanded by one of Dingane's most trusted indunas, Ndela KaOmpisi. He had five regiments at his disposal; both the uDlangezwa and the iziNyosi were experienced warriors. They were brigaded with the younger uMkhulutshane. All three regiments were based at uMgungundlovu (and probably smaller units were attached to the three regiments). The remainder of the force was drawn from the raw and recently raised uDlambedlu and the uKhokhoti.

The Zulu force encamped in the hills overlooking the Ncome on the night of 15 December. The Voortrekkers, aware of the immediate presence of the Zulu, slept fitfully that night. Ndela KaOmpisi set his men in motion before dawn on 16 December. The younger men took up the horn positions to the left and right, aiming directly at each of the drifts.

By dawn the uDlambedlu were deployed within 200 metres of the laager, on the western side of the river. The bulk of the rest of the Zulu force was still up to a mile away, but closing fast. Before the rest of the army was in position, the uDlambedlu rose to attack the laager. As the uDlambedlu closed to within 80 metres, the Voortrekkers opened fire with a variety of muskets and rudimentary shotguns, supported by the devastating canister of a cannon.

The uDlambedlu were thrown back with huge casualties at least six times; many had slipped into the Donga to escape the galling fire. Pretorius sent out a mounted patrol to winkle the Zulu out of the Donga. The attack and pursuit achieved the purpose of breaking the uDlambedlu, who were now effectively out of the battle. By now the uMkhulutshane had reached the more northerly drift, appearing and then disappearing in the undulating terrain. Pretorius recalled his mounted contingent and placed them on the western side of the drift to catch the Zulu as they tried to cross.

As the uMkhulutshane stormed across the drift, the Voortrekkers opened fire. The regiment could make no headway and retired to the south where the uDlangezwa and the iziNyosi were approaching the lower drift in preparation to cross. Around this time Pretorius ordered one of the cannons to open fire on the Zulu commanders and the reserve regiment, the uKhokhoti. This caused enormous confusion and some casualties.

Meanwhile, the uMkhulutshane were taking up positions vacated by the routed uDlambedlu. Despite several brave attempts to close on the laager, they too were beaten back and soon were retreating in disorder. With the Zulu chest regiments (the uDlangezwa and the iziNyosi) closing, they launched disorganized attacks against the laager with no better results. Each time an attack developed it was cut down and decimated by concentrated Voortrekker fire.

The initiative had now been lost and Pretorius sought to take full advantage of the situation and finish the shattered and dispirited Zulu. He ordered the bulk of the men to mount and ride out to mop up any Zulu resistance. With the Voortrekkers in pursuit, some Zulu fled to the north (to a hill

75

which became known as Vegkop), or attempted to reach the lower drift and slip away to the south.

The Voortrekkers showed no mercy and slaughtered all that came within range. Dozens were shot as they tried to cross the river or hide in the reed banks. In short order the whole Zulu force was routed. The battle had lasted barely two hours, but around 3,000 Zulu had perished, both in the ruinous assaults on the laager, but more in the pursuit. Voortrekker casualties amounted to just three wounded, one of whom was Pretorius, who had suffered a hand wound from a spear. Pretorius could now advance on eMgungundlovu and seize Dingane, if he could be found.

The Boers reached uMgungundlovu on 20 December 1838, but Dingane had already abandoned his kraal and had built a new one on the northern bank of the Black Mfolozi River. The Boers had to content themselves with looting what remained of the kraal and burying the bones of Retief and his men. On 27 December a Boer patrol rode into the uPathe Valley, led by a Zulu deserter, Bhongoza kaMefu; it was a trap and the Boers did not encounter the promised cattle, but a Zulu ambush. Amongst the five settlers and several servants killed was Alexander Biggar.

In March 1839 Dingane agreed to make peace with the Boers, allowing them to settle in Natal and paying them an enormous cattle fine. Dingane proposed to compensate himself for the loss of Natal by launching a new campaign against the Swazi, but despite the best efforts of the Zulu army, it ended in failure.

However, whilst Dingane's attention was focussed on the Swazi, Mpande kaSenzangakhona crossed the Thukela River at the head of 17,000 Zulu and over 25,000 cattle. He took with him Nongalaza kaNondela and Zulu kaNogandaya. It was a move which would become known as the breaking of the rope, referring to the sacred coil which bound the Zulu nation. Mpande created an uneasy alliance with the Boers and proposed that with their assistance he would overthrow Dingane.

The combined force crossed the Thukela on 18 January 1840.

Peace negotiations had failed between Dingane, represented by his chief minister, Dambusa kaSobadli. Ultimately the Boers had clapped him in irons and taken him with them on their advance. The entire force of Boers, under Pretorius, amounted to some 400 men and Mpande was accompanied by Nongalaza kaNondela at the head of 5,000 warriors. The column's first port of call, eleven days later, was the battlefield at the Ncome River. Dambusa was tried before a kangaroo court in Dingane's absence for the murder of Retief and was sentenced to death by firing squad.

Meanwhile, Nongalaza had advanced into northern Zululand and encountered Dingane's army, under Ndlela, near Magudo in the Maqongqo Hills. Dingane had been caught in the process of retreating from his second royal kraal, but his army turned and fought well against Mpande's troops. Although very little is known about the battle itself, upwards of 1,000 fell on either side. Such must have been the ferocity of the battle that a Boer reported that Nongalaza's troops had suffered 1,200 wounded.

So far, despite the promises and the punitive reparations demanded by Pretorius and the Boers, they had contributed absolutely nothing to overthrowing Dingane. Pretorius and the Boers were more concerned in gathering up Zulu cattle; they had already appropriated 30,000 and in addition they had taken 1,000 Zulu children to become Boer slaves.

Dingane had fled through Pongolo and then into the lands controlled by the Swazi. He had been all but deserted by his people, yet Ndlela remained faithful. Dingane, remembering that Ndlela had spoken eloquently to spare Mpande from the royal cull which had occurred in the aftermath of Shaka's death, put the old man to death. Ndlela had had a vital role to play in Zulu history; he had single-handedly ensured that Senzangakhona's lineage would rule the Zulu.

Ultimately Dingane met his own end at the hands of a sub-clan of the Swazi, the Nyawo. He was murdered and his body interred as befitted a king. Mpande would succeed his elder brother, but not before the Boers had extracted yet another 8,000 cattle in payment for his coronation.

Chapter Six

Mpande kaSenzangakhona and the Zulu Civil War

The Boers proclaimed Mpande king of the Zulu on 10 February 1840, before Dingane was even dead. The Boers had appropriated over 60,000 cattle and a further 8,000, which they extracted from Mpande for proclaiming him king, only added to the total Zulu losses.

After Dingane's death, Zulu refugees, who had fled during his rule, began to flood back into the Natal region. Thousands of Zulu were resettling their abandoned kraals which caused insurmountable problems for the Boers who had been given farms in Natal. In December 1840 Pretorius decided to move against the clans that had been taking back cattle from the Boers. At the head of 200 men he rode along the south of the Drakensberg Range. The trail led him to the amaBaca clan, led by their chieftain, Ncapaai; Pretorius wiped them out and snatched back the cattle.

This move sent shockwaves through the Cape colony and Sir George Napier had already been instructed by the Colonial Office in London to reoccupy Durban. At first he chose to delay acting on the order, but when Faku, the chief of the amaMpondo, complained to the British that the Boers were evicting Zulu and forcing them into his territory, Napier realized he would have to act. Napier had very few troops to deploy; the closest men to Durban occupied a fort in amaMpondoland. Consequently, Captain Thomas Charlton Smith, at the head of 263 men (two companies of the 27th, a detachment of the Royal Engineers, some Cape Mounted Rifles and a handful of artillerymen) and 250 servants, with sixty wagons, began the 150 mile journey in April 1842. It was no mean feat that Smith was facing, as he had over 120 rivers to cross.

By 4 May Smith had established a stockade protected by a howitzer and two field guns barely a mile from Durban. On 23 May, after provocation from the Boers, Smith led his command to attack them. Pretorius deployed his men amongst mangrove trees and the result of the sharp fight cost the British twenty dead and thirty-one wounded; Pretorius had lost just a single man. Effectively Smith was now under siege.

Smith sent Dick King (a fluent Zulu speaker who had been in Natal since 1828) to Grahamstown, 600 miles south, to inform the British of his plight. Accompanied by a sixteen year old Zulu, Ndongeni, he managed the trip in just ten days. A single company of the 27th immediately boarded a vessel and headed up the coast. Meanwhile, Pretorius had surrounded Smith with 600 men, but all attempts to storm the fort failed. By mid-June, with the siege having lasted over thirty days, the company from Grahamstown arrived, supported by five further companies of the 25th, who landed from HMS *Southampton*. Pretorius made one last attempt to overrun the fort but failed and retreated. The companies of the 25th were commanded by Colonel Josias Cloete. He immediately set about confiscating cattle from all the local Boer homesteads.

Mpande contacted Cloete and offered to muster his regiments to storm Pietermaritzburg (the Boer capital), but his offer was politely turned down. Mpande had realized that Dingane had already signed a treaty with the British which effectively overrode any arrangements he had been forced to make with the Boers. The Boers were in a desperate situation; Cloete made the trip to Pietermaritzburg and told them that they must submit to the British, return all captured property and prisoners and hand over any Boers who had been implicated in looting. The Boers had no option and submitted. Cloete and the 25th then left for Afghanistan and Smith, now a Major, was based in Durban with 350 men and eight artillery pieces.

This action between the Boers and the British had done little to solve the problems between the Boers and the Zulu. Both groups were raiding and counter-raiding one another for cattle and squabbling over land. Ultimately the British decided that Natal should become a colony and Cloete's brother, Henry, was appointed High Commissioner, arriving in Durban on 5 June 1843. Henry Cloete faced a difficult situation; many of the Boers were simply refusing to cooperate, so from Durban he called for 200 reinforcements. After much argument and deliberation, the Boers conceded to annexation and Natal became part of the British Empire on 31 August 1843.

Cloete made his first visit to Mpande in the September, demanding that the Zulu monarch cede St Lucia Bay to the British and that Mpande should recognize that the Zulu kingdom ended at the Thukela River and the Buffalo River. Mpande finally agreed on 5 October. On 12 December 1845 Natal officially became a British colony and Martin West was appointed the first Lieutenant Governor.

By 1845 there were at least 40,000 refugees in the Natal area. This was compounded in 1848 by the arrival of the amaHlubi, who been driven out of Zululand and settled amongst the Drakensberg Range. In 1849, James Rorke acquired a 3,000 acre farm on the Buffalo River. He built a thatched house just ten miles to the west of Zululand. Rorke was a typical settler and served in the Buffalo Border Guard. When he died in 1875 the farm was acquired by Otto Witt, who converted a storehouse into a chapel. Even then the significance of Rorke's estate could not be guessed.

The diplomatic agent to the natives was Theophilus Shepstone, who set about dividing sections of Natal into eight reserves for the growing black population. Some 80,000 natives were moved into these reserves which would have their own magistrate, mission stations and a police force. Significantly, in 1850, the Lieutenant Governor of Natal was proclaimed Supreme Chief of the native population, which effectively cut Mpande from being able to exercise any control over the clans to which he was still nominally their king.

Meanwhile, across the Thukela River, the Zulu kingdom, under the comparatively placid rule of Mpande, had recovered from the losses of both cattle and prestige inflicted upon them by the Boers. Mpande had established his royal kraal on the White Umfolozi River at kwaNodwengu.

Mpande chose not to meddle or exercise direct control over local decisions, leaving these to the clan chieftains. Mpande was around forty-four years old (born 1796) when he became monarch. He was to produce twenty-nine sons and thirty daughters from his twenty or more wives. He had taken his first wife, Ngqumbhazi, daughter of Manzini, in 1825. Ngqumbhazi had already been married and had a son when she and Mpande wed. Shaka had had the boy killed when he objected to the marriage and had also arranged the marriage of Mpande to Monase. She also had a son who was also killed by Shaka. By the time Mpande was twenty-one he was married, therefore, to two childless widows. Mpande's first born by Ngqumbhazi was Cetshwayo in 1827. Very soon after Cetshwayo's birth Monase also bore him a son, Mbuyazi. Ngqumbhazi would provide him with three sons; Monase four sons and three daughters.

According to Zulu tradition the first born son was not normally the heir to the throne. The heir would be the eldest son of a man's Great Wife. Mpande never appointed a Great Wife, but technically speaking, since Ngqumbhazi was Mpande's first wife, Cetshwayo was not his heir. As it would transpire, Mbuyazi had an equal claim to the throne, if not a better one than Cetshwayo. Back in 1839 Mpande had presented Cetshwayo to the Boers as his heir. Bizarrely, the Boers had clipped a piece of Cetshwayo's ear in order to ensure that they would recognize him as the heir in future years.

Mpande was acutely aware of the fact that each successive king had taken the throne by force and was keen to avoid either Cetshwayo or Mbuyazi forming a power base that would allow them to do the same thing. Ngqumbhazi was sent with her children to the north of the Black Umfolozi River, to the kwaGqikazi kraal, whilst Cetshwayo was sent to the royal kraal at emLambongwenya (near Eshowe). Monase and her children were likewise dispatched to a distant kraal, as was Mbuyazi.

81

Cetshwayo lost no time in beginning to forge alliances and links with powerful groups, both within the kingdom and without. He established a rapport with the boys who were already being called up into the kwaGqikazi and also the Mandlakazi to the west and the Buthelezi to the south.

In 1850 Mpande had created the Uthulwana regiment; both Cetshwayo and Mbuyazi were recruited into the regiment. It was commanded by the Buthelezi chieftain and close friend of Mpande, Mnyamana kaNgqengele. Both of the princes were present in 1852 when the Uthulwana were deployed against the Swazi. It is said that from an early age Cetshwayo showed considerable bravery and skill in battle and that he had dealt with a Swazi patrol single-handedly. Cetshwayo had begun to draw around him a group of men who called themselves uSuthu. This may seem to have been an odd choice, as the name was derived from an incident in 1851 when Mpande's army captured thousands of long-horned Sotho cattle from the Bapedi. The name inferred a vast herd and military strength. Meanwhile, Mbuyazi had begun to draw around him his own followers who called themselves iziGqoza which meant to trickle like drops of water, referring to the slow but steady number of supporters flocking to Mbuyazi's support.

Mpande must have been concerned as to the numbers of supporters flocking to the royal princes. Whether he feared that the princes would clash with one another, or ultimately would challenge his own throne is unclear. But he took immediate steps to try to cut them both from their power bases. Cetshwayo was ordered to establish a royal kraal at oNdini (Ulundi) near Eshowe. This was in the south-east of Zululand. Mbuyazi, on the other hand, was told to establish a kraal on the White Umfolozi River. This now meant that Mpande's own royal kraal, kwaNodwengu, separated the two princes. If Mpande had hoped that this action would have prevented the inevitable, he was mistaken, and indeed by his own action, on one particular occasion, he seems to have only fuelled the rivalry between the two princes.

Mpande called both of the princes to a ceremony where he was to present them with new shields. Traditionally the most powerful, and therefore the most coveted shield, bore the mark of the spear which had killed the cattle. He had intended to give it to Cetshwayo, but at the last moment he decided to give it to Mbuyazi. This incident is suggested by many to be the final act which made conflict inevitable.

In early 1856 both Cetshwayo and Mbuyazi requested that Mpande give them permission to hunt at the meeting point of the Black and White Umfolozi Rivers. It seems clear that the hunt was a ruse and that they intended to fight one another. Mbuyazi had planned to arrive at the point where he had agreed to meet Cetshwayo before his rival, but as it transpired Cetshwayo arrived there first and had considerably more men with him than Mbuyazi. Consequently, on this occasion Mbuyazi backed down. Mpande received word of this near confrontation and was even more desperate to take steps to avoid what appeared increasingly to be the inevitable.

There seemed to be no other solution as far as Mpande was concerned; he took steps to persuade Mbuyazi to occupy an area just to the north of the Thukela River. This was the same tract of land which Mpande had occupied during Dingane's reign. It gave Mbuyazi and his supporters the opportunity to slip across the border into Natal, just as Mpande had done. This new move placed Mbuyazi very close to Cetshwayo's own kraal, oNdini, and Cetshwayo began to mobilize for fear that Mbuyazi would attack him.

Mbuyazi, by the November it appears, was intent upon crossing into Natal and was already beginning negotiations with the white settlers to support him. With war seemingly imminent in the Thukela region, white traders, their families and cattle began making their way to the lower drift on the river, only to discover that the rain had made it impossible to cross. Mbuyazi managed to enlist the support of John Dunn, son of Robert Dunn. John Dunn worked for the Colonial Border agent, Captain Joshua Walmesley and against Walmesley's express orders, crossed the river to offer his services. Most of Dunn's followers were trained hunters and called themselves the iziMqobo (the crushers).

Battle focus

Ndondakusuka

2 December 1856

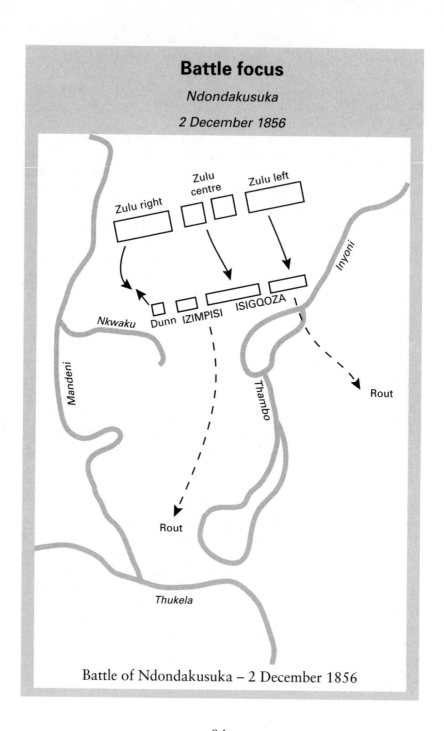

Battle of Ndondakusuka – 2 December 1856

Cetshwayo's army amounted to some 15–20,000 men and by 30 November they were encamped in the Mandeni Valley, only a short distance from Mbuyazi's iziGqoza. Cetshwayo's main force was his uSuthu followers, in the form of the regiments, the uDlambedlu, iSangqu, uThulwana, iNdlondlo, Ndabakwombe, uDloko and the izinGulube. This core was supported by the abaQulusi, Maphitha's Mandlakazi and troops from the tribes Zungu, Mdlalose and Cube.

Mbuyazi could muster around 7,000 warriors, in addition to which John Dunn provided 200 trained hunters, mainly from his own retinue, but with some whites (many of whom were traders). Mbuyazi's men could be distinguished from the more regular forces under Cetshwayo by two strips of cowhide worn on their headdresses with attached cow tails. Mbuyazi was generally bereft of experienced commanders or troops, but notably he had the support of one of Mpande's favoured Indunas, Nongalaza kaNondela. At dawn on 2 December Cetshwayo's army advanced out of the Mandeni Valley towards the hills known as Masomongca. From here they could see Mbuyazi's men deployed on a ridge facing them. The battlefield encompassed the very site which had seen Mpande's army eliminate the Grand Army of Natal in 1838.

Cetshwayo's chest comprised of the uDloko, izinGulube, iNdabakawombe, the Mdlalose, Cube and abaQulusi. The right horn included the uDlambedlu, iSangqu, the uThulwana and the iNdlondo, whilst the left horn comprised the Mandlakazi and the Zungu.

The left wing of Mbuyazi's army was fixed to a stream, known as the Nkwaku. Before Cetshwayo's army closed to attack, two inauspicious events befell Mbuyazi. Firstly, Cetshwayo had captured one of Mbuyazi's war shields, which he threw to the ground and knelt on. This displayed Cetshwayo's invincibility. Around the same time an ostrich feather fell from Mbuyazi's headdress, which could only mean that the outcome of the battle had already been preordained.

In terms of weaponry, the bulk of Cetshwayo's army was traditionally armed. Few of the men had muskets, although Cetshwayo had given command of one of the horns to a Boer called Christian Groening. As Cetshwayo's army closed, it became clear that his right horn was aiming to outflank Dunn, who was positioned on the far left of Mbuyazi's army. Dunn moved his troops, along with the iziMpisi (led by Mbuyazi's brother, Shonkweni kaMpande). Dunn's troops delivered devastating fire into the oncoming right horn, forcing them to fall back. Cetshwayo realized that this weighty attack had failed and threw his left horn against Mbuyazi's right. This time the Mandlakazi and the Zungu managed to charge home and threw the iziGqoza back in disorder across the iNyoni. Cetshwayo's left, ably led by Matsheni and Sikazana, had shattered Mbuyazi's line; the centre could have no hope of standing in its position and Mbuyazi ordered his men to retire and Cetshwayo threw his chest at the enemy. To begin with the retreat was carefully paced, but Dunn, on Mbuyazi's left, was finding it increasingly difficult to prevent Cetshwayo's right horn from overlapping him and cutting him off from the Thukela River. The retreat soon degenerated into a rout with the uSuthu slaughtering everyone within spear distance, including the iziGqoza civilians.

Dunn's men managed to retain a semblance of order at least until he reached the banks of the Thukela. On the island in the middle of the river were the bulk of the white civilians and non-combatants. The uSuthu did not attack them, yet many of the whites perished in the river in their terror, along with the iziGqoza warriors and civilians many of whom fell prey to the crocodiles.

Somewhere amidst the chaos Mbuyazi was killed, as was Shonkweni and five other sons of Mpande. It is believed that between 15 and 20,000 iziGqoza were slaughtered, only 5,000 of whom were warriors. Dunn survived, but most of his retainers were dead. Precisely how many uSuthu died is difficult to assess, but it was undoubtedly considerably fewer and may not have exceeded 1,000 men.

1. A Zulu chieftain with his tribal warriors, possibly taken at the beginning of the twentieth century. Warriors have a variety of different shield designs and wear cow tail regalia.

2. Two Zulu warriors beside their beehive hut; one carries the knobkerrie.

3. A later period Zulu warrior with smaller ceremonial shield.

4. An early twentieth century posed shot of a married chieftain. Note the typical strips of animal fur around his loins.

5. Three older Zulus. Note the headband signifying them as married men.

6. A posed ceremonial dance. Most of the warriors seem to be without shields but carry knobkerries.

7. A later period view of a Zulu regiment. The induna carries a knobkerrie and is wearing leopard skin. The shields are predominantly white with brown patches.

8. A late period posed photograph with a variety of shields and very stylised knobkerries.

9. A mixed group showing possibly two generations of Zulu in their kraal.

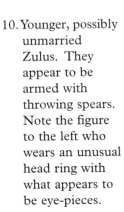

10. Younger, possibly unmarried Zulus. They appear to be armed with throwing spears. Note the figure to the left who wears an unusual head ring with what appears to be eye-pieces.

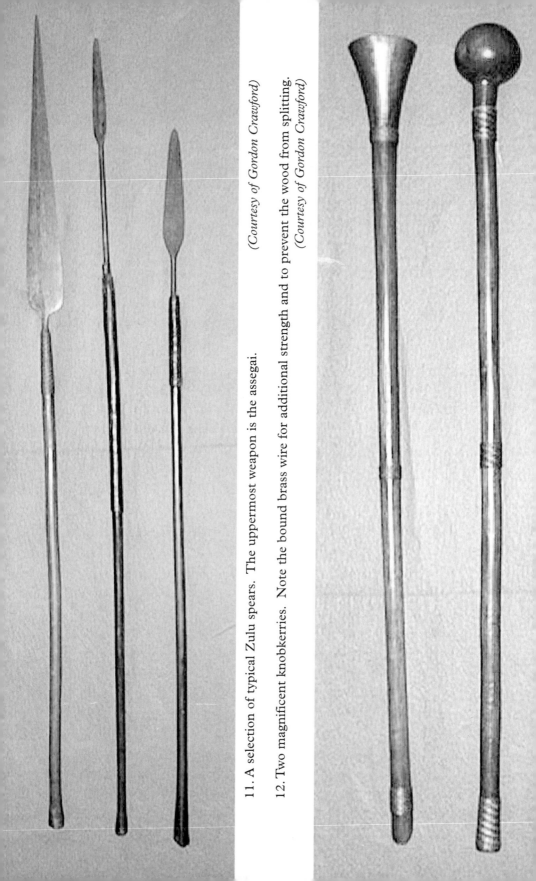

11. A selection of typical Zulu spears. The uppermost weapon is the assegai.

(*Courtesy of Gordon Crawford*)

12. Two magnificent knobkerries. Note the bound brass wire for additional strength and to prevent the wood from splitting.

(*Courtesy of Gordon Crawford*)

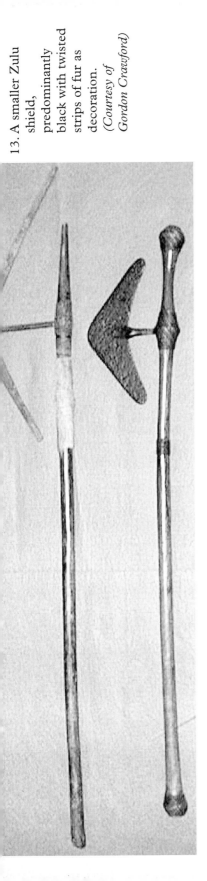

13. A smaller Zulu
    shield,
    predominantly
    black with twisted
    strips of fur as
    decoration.
    *(Courtesy of
    Gordon Crawford)*

14. Two comparatively
    rare Zulu axes. The
    lower example
    appears to be a
    converted knobkerrie.
    *(Courtesy of Gordon
    Crawford)*

15 A relatively contemporary photograph of a Zulu kraal illustrating the structure of the beehive huts.

16. A contemporary Zulu kraal showing beehive huts and surrounding wooden palisade.
(Courtesy of Gordon Crawford)

17. Two old and elaborate snuff holders made of horn, typically worn around the neck.
(Courtesy of Gordon Crawford)

18. A contemporary photograph of Zulu warriors with a wide variety of weapons, shield types and clothing and regalia made from a number of different furs.

(Courtesy of Gordon Crawford)

19. A contemporary picture of a Zulu with ceremonial costume. Unlike his predecessors, he wears sandals.

(Courtesy of Gordon Crawford)

20. A frontal view of a contemporary Zulu in ceremonial costume with small, beige shield with black strips and an ornate knobkerrie.

(Courtesy of Gordon Crawford)

21. Tshaneni; a view taken from the peak.

(Courtesy of Stephen Coan, The Witness)

22. The peak on the left is Gaza and Tshaneni is on the right.
(Courtesy of Stephen Coan, The Witness)

23. The iSiphezi Valley.   *(Courtesy of Mo at the 1879 Group)*

24. Four members of the 1879 Group at the reconstructed site of Rorke's Drift. *(Courtesy of Mo at the 1879 Group)*

25. The Mizinyathi Valley. *(Courtesy of Mo at the 1879 Group)*

26. A member of the 1879 Group on the battlefield at Isandlwana. Note the white-washed cairns marking the place where the dead were found.

(Courtesy of Mo at the 1879 Group)

27. The 1879 Group at Isandlwana. The shape of the Isandlwana hill in the rear is reminiscent of the sphinx symbol on the 24 Infantry Regiment's badge.

(Courtesy of Mo at the 1879 Group)

28. The memorial to the fallen members of the 24 Regiment at Isandlwana.

(Courtesy of Mo at the 1879 Group)

29. Typical countryside in Zululand. Note the tall elephant grass and the escarpment to the rear. *(Courtesy of Mo at the 1879 Group)*

30. 1879 re-enactors in a single rank, delivering a volley with their Martini-Henry rifles. *(Courtesy of Mo at the 1879 Group)*

For a short while it appeared that Cetshwayo would lead his army across the river and fall on the almost unprotected Natal. But instead he withdrew.

The traders operating in Zululand had lost the bulk of their cattle and were furious with Dunn that his involvement in the battle had led to Cetshwayo appropriating the beasts. Dunn offered to settle the situation himself; if he was successful he would not only make a friend of Cetshwayo, but also obtain the reward which had been offered for the cattle. He first headed to meet with Mpande. The frightened king willingly met with him and Dunn was thanked for his assistance and the news about the death of several of Mpande's sons. Dunn then headed for Cetshwayo's kraal. He managed to strike up friendly relations and, after just three days, he had won Cetshwayo's friendship and retrieved the cattle for the traders.

Not long afterwards Cetshwayo asked Dunn to settle near the coastal area to the north of the Thukela River as a chieftain. It was a bizarre opportunity and Dunn in effect would rule over several kraals with a population of 10,000. Cetshwayo needed Dunn to act as an advisor and negotiator with the British and the Boer. He was already married but this did not stop Dunn from behaving just as a Zulu chieftain would do; he would ultimately boast forty-nine wives and 116 children.

Mpande's situation was now fully undermined and in effect, even though Mpande was still king, Cetshwayo ruled the kingdom. Cetshwayo was still not fully recognized by Mpande as his successor, however. Cetshwayo wiped out one of Mpande's wive's families, Nomanshali, in 1860. Mpande's wife and her daughters were killed and the two eldest sons escaped to Transvaal. The youngest son, Mpoyana, was tracked down and taken to Mpande's kraal where he was killed before the monarch's eyes.

One of the sons who had escaped into Transvaal was Mtonga, a favourite of Mpande. He was in the Utrecht district of the Transvaal, an area ceded to the Boers five years earlier. Cetshwayo approached the Boer representatives in the district, offering them land in return for Mtonga. In March 1861 the deal was done and Cetshwayo signed away a strip of land between the Buffalo and Blood Rivers, almost as far as the home which Rorke had established beside the drift on the Buffalo River. Cetshwayo agreed that he would not kill Mtonga or his brother and, in the same accord known as the Treaty of Waaihoek, he agreed that he would not challenge his father or make any aggressive expansionist moves. The agreement and particularly the exchange of land, which had been endorsed by Mpande, alarmed the British, specifically Theophilus Shepstone. He realized that ultimately the Boers would seek to expand into Zululand and, perhaps, annexe the territory. He was determined that should the Zulu be crushed, that Natal would take Zululand and not the Boers.

With Mtonga effectively out of the picture, as far as Cetshwayo was concerned there were still at least four other potential heirs to Mpande's throne. Two half-brothers were in hiding in Natal and a third, Uhamu, was difficult to find as he was well hidden in the north of the country. There remained a fourth potential heir, Mkungo, who was also in Natal at Bishopstowe, just 16 kilometres east of Pietermaritzburg. In July 1861 a panic swept Natal as rumours spread that Cetshwayo was about to unleash an army to snatch Mkungo.

Shepstone realized the precarious position Natal was in and that it could quite easily become a battlefield in the political machinations of the Zulu court. He made for Mpande's kraal at kaNodwengu. Mpande was fully aware of the peril that his people would be placed under if Cetshwayo violated Natal's borders. He therefore offered to name Cetshwayo as his heir. Cetshwayo was summoned and Mpande announced his decision and Shepstone, for what it was worth, pledged Natal's support. At least some of Cetshwayo's advisors warned him that neither Shepstone nor Natal had any business in meddling with the Zulu succession. Shepstone did not improve the situation by telling Cetshwayo that once he had succeeded to the throne, Natal would not allow him to be an unjust ruler. It was to be an early sign to Cetshwayo that the British did, indeed, wish to control the destiny of the Zulu.

The situation was at least temporarily diffused and Cetshwayo would eventually succeed Mpande. But in 1864, Mtonga fled to Natal and Shepstone, considering that he might be useful to him at some future date, refused to send him home. Meanwhile the

Boers of Transvaal, led by Pretorius, sought to ensure that the treaty which they had signed with Cetshwayo and Mpande would be free of any misunderstandings. With the assistance of the Zulu chieftain, Sihayo (who would figure heavily in the early stages of the Anglo-Zulu War of 1879) they erected a series of cairns along the new boundary to the east of the Blood River. The Boer delegation was led by Pretorius.

Mpande died in October 1872; he was the last of Senzanga-khona's sons. He had ruled for thirty-two years and during that time there had only been one major upheaval which had cost him the lives of several of his sons, as well as Mbuyazi. Mpande had steered a nation which had reeled from the rapacious Boers back to a powerful, military state, with even more men potentially under arms than Shaka could ever have imagined. Each man from his late teens to his sixties was part of a regiment. Mpande was the only son of Senzangakhona to have died of natural causes; the other eleven had met with violent deaths at the hands of brothers or others.

Even with Mpande dead and his succession seemingly assured, Cetshwayo was still uncertain. His uSuthu were still not the strongest military force in the kingdom. Uhamu lived in an area which fell within the territory ceded under the Treaty of Waaihoek. In the interim Mpande and Cetshwayo had repudiated the treaty and returned the purchase price to the Boers. Nonetheless, there were several dozen Boer homesteads and even more Zulu kraals in what was to become the disputed territory. Cetshwayo's ally, Maphitha, had died and had been succeeded by his son, Usibebu. Undoubtedly Usibebu controlled the strongest faction in Zululand and it was not clear who he was prepared to support. To add to Cetshwayo's concerns was the rumour that Mbuyazi had survived the battle of Ndondakusuka (despite the fact that Cetshwayo had ordered that he was to be flayed alive and crucified after the battle if he had not been killed). Cetshwayo turned to Dunn and told him that he wished him to leave for Natal and obtain as many guns as possible. He returned with 150 rifles and several hundred others would follow. If nothing else, Cetshwayo believed that this would strengthen the uSuthu in any possible civil war.

By the beginning of 1873, with Cetshwayo still not installed as king, much against his better judgement he approached Shepstone as representative of the British to crown him King of the Zulu in the name of the Queen of England. Shepstone was delighted, as this would bring the Zulu into the British fold and, perhaps, give the British the opportunity of being able to occupy the disputed territory, creating a buffer zone between the Zulu and the Transvaal.

Consequently, Shepstone, at the head of Victoria, Alexandra and Richmond Mounted Rifles (amounting to just over 100 men), along with two artillery pieces of the Durban Volunteer Artillery and a brass band, entered the Zulu kingdom to perform the ceremony.

Chapter Seven

Cetshwayo kaMpande
1873 – February 1879

On 1 September 1873 Shepstone, in the name of Queen Victoria, placed a tinsel crown on Cetshwayo's head and named him the Zulu King. Not content with this, Shepstone proposed to apply Native Customary Law of Natal upon the Zulu. Henceforth, Shepstone proclaimed, no Zulu would be killed without a trial and witnesses and even then he would have the right of appeal to the king. No Zulu would be killed without the king's consent and crimes which had incurred the death penalty would be replaced with cattle fines.

Cetshwayo had absolutely no intention of accepting these demands. Nonetheless, he could not ignore the fact that both economically and in terms of population, Natal had already outstripped Zululand and his territory was replete with white traders offering trinkets in return for the life blood of the nation; their cattle.

Cetshwayo established his royal kraal at oNdini (Ulundi), a vast, sprawling settlement in which 300,000 Zulu lived. Twelve regimental kraals were established in the immediate vicinity of the Mahlabathini Plain.

Southern Africa, in terms of British ambition, had radically changed. During the 1860s diamonds had been discovered near Kimberley. There was now a distinct reason for the British to invest in the region. Equally, it became clear that the juggernaut of 'civilization' should not be impeded by a backward Boer republic, or indeed by the Zulu. Centralized government was seen as the answer and in April 1877 the British annexed the Transvaal. Together with a drought in the same year, there was now intense pressure to occupy the disputed territory which both Cetshwayo and Mpande had agreed, but which Cetshwayo now repudiated.

The new British High Commissioner, Sir Henry Bartle Frere, was appointed by the Colonial Office. His remit was to achieve confederation and from the outset Shepstone, having originally supported the Zulu claim to the disputed territory, had now thrown his weight behind the Boers of Transvaal now that they were under British influence.

Cetshwayo had made no less than eighteen applications to have the border dispute discussed in arbitration (between 1861 and 1876). Mpande had even proposed that the bulk of the disputed land be ceded to Natal to act as a buffer zone in 1869. The matter had to be resolved.

Frere appointed a Boundary Commission to investigate the disputed territory and to his enormous surprise, the commission backed the Zulu claim. It met at Rorke's Drift on 7 March 1878, headed by the Attorney General of Natal, Michael H. Gallwey. The other two members of the commission were Shepstone's brother, John and Lieutenant Colonel William Anthony Durnford, of the Royal Artillery. After five weeks' deliberation, during which the commission listened to the sketchy memories and somewhat selective ones of various witnesses, Gallwey recommended that the whole of the Blood River area, including Utrecht, be returned to the ownership of the Zulu. The report was completed on 20 June 1878. Frere, however, was determined to find a justification to attack the Zulu.

On 28 October 1878 he wrote:

> I can only repeat my own conviction that the continued preservation of peace depends no longer on what the servants of the British Government here may do or abstain from doing, but simply on the caprice of an ignorant and blood-thirsty despot, with an organised force of at least 40,000 armed men at his absolute command.

Theoretically at least, Cetshwayo did have some 40,000 men to call upon, but of the twenty-six regiments all but four dated from Mpande's time or before. Cetshwayo had only created four new regiments. Of greater concern was the fact that only eighteen of the regiments had been given permission to marry and traditionally the men would not be given permission to marry until they had proved themselves in battle. In September 1876 the uDloko and the iNdolondlo had been sent to punish the Tonga tribe. This then gave Cetshwayo the opportunity to allow them to marry. He told them that they could marry women from the inGcugce, a female age group somewhat younger than themselves. Many of these women had already taken younger husbands and Cetshwayo decreed that if any of the inGcugce were found living with a man less than forty years of age, she was to be killed and her father's cattle confiscated. Some women were, indeed, killed but others pretended to marry the elder brothers of the men that they had already married. More, however, fled into Natal or Transvaal. The British sent a terse message to Cetshwayo, reminding him that he had agreed to outlaw summary executions; the monarch was furious.

The incident with the inGcugce caused a rift with Hamu, who was the induna of the uThulwana. In January 1878 the uThulwana were barracked with the iNgobamakhosi for the impending ceremonies. The iNgobamakhosi had lost several wives and lovers to older men. They were also outraged at the fact that some young men had been incorporated into the uThulwana, thereby giving them the same rights as their older colleagues in the uThulwana. The two regiments got into a vicious stick fight which degenerated into utter chaos, leaving some sixty warriors dead. Hamu, as the induna of the uThulwana and the brother of Cetshwayo, demanded that the monarch summarily execute Sigcwelecwele, the induna of the iNgobamakhosi. Cetshwayo refused and the disgruntled Hamu led his regiment away towards the Transvaal border. Cetshwayo was concerned that he would lose the support of his brother and agreed to kill Sigcwelecwele. John Dunn, whose camp had seen the worst of the fighting between the two regiments, managed to persuade Cetshwayo at the eleventh hour simply to fine Sigcwelecwele, for fear that his killing would further inflame the situation.

Two other incidents brought additional ammunition for Frere in 1878. Mbilini, who claimed the Swazi throne, offered and had accepted his allegiance to Cetshwayo, but Mbilini raided the Zulu, Swazi and Boers for cattle. This made Cetshwayo ultimately responsible for Mbilini's actions. The Boers demanded that Cetshwayo turn Mbilini over to them, but the monarch refused and sent 100 cattle to the Boers by means of compensation. Mbilini continued to raid indiscriminately and Cetshwayo had to cast him adrift.

Perhaps the most significant incident occurred in July 1878. The Zulu induna, Sihayo Ka Xongo, lived a short distance from Rorke's Drift. Two of Sihayo's wives, including his Great Wife, Kaqwelebana, had taken younger lovers. Sihayo was with the king in oNdini and Kaqwelebana's eldest son, Mhlokazulu, discovered that his mother was being unfaithful. In consultation with his father's brother, Zuluhlenga, and three of his brothers, Bhekuzulu, Mkumbikazulu and Shenkwana, resolved to kill Kaqwelebana. They attempted to kill her, but only succeeded in wounding her. Both women and their lovers slipped across the border into Natal, but foolishly they only chose to hide in a kraal just a short distance inside Natal. Mhlokazulu and Zuluhlenga slipped across the river, kidnapped Sihayo's younger wife and brought her back into Zululand, murdering her there.

Several days later Mhlokazulu discovered where his own mother was hiding. He crossed the river with thirty mounted Zulu, including his uncle and three brothers. They were supported by fifty more Zulu on foot. Kaqwelebana was hiding in a kraal owned by the border guard called Maziyana. The Great Wife was seized, taken back across the river and shot.

In truth there was no way that Cetshwayo could have known any of this. None of the deaths had taken place in Natal and no one had been harmed in Natal. The British objected in the strongest possible terms to the violation of their territory.

On 16 November the British informed Cetshwayo that the outcome of the Boundary Commission would be announced at the lower drift of the Thukela River on 11 December. The British would be there in force, occupying an earthwork fort overlooking the drift, manned by 170 sailors and marines. The complement was complete with two artillery pieces and a Gatling gun. Three indunas and several chieftains and retainers represented Cetshwayo, and John Shepstone began to read the report of the Boundary Commission. Frere had made some significant changes; whilst the Zulu were granted their rights over the disputed territory, the Boers who had farms in the area would have the choice to either leave, in which case the Zulu would have to compensate them, or they would stay under the protection of the British.

The Zulu representatives, including John Dunn, made ready to leave, but Shepstone asked them to remain and have lunch. He then read out his brother's ultimatum. There were no less than thirteen points. The first three required Cetshwayo to adhere within twenty days. Sihayo's brother and his three sons were to face charges in the Natal court. Cetshwayo was to pay 500 head of cattle for Mhlokazulu's violation of Natal territory. He would also have to pay an additional 100 cattle for an incident which had occurred some time before, when two surveyors had been temporarily detained by some Zulu in the course of inspecting the terrain leading to a drift on the Thukela. The other ten points of the ultimatum were all the more serious.

First, Mbilini was to be turned over to be tried in the Transvaal courts. The second point reiterated the demand that no Zulu were to be executed without trial and appeal to the king. The remaining seven points cut to the very heart of the Zulu way of life. The regimental system was to be abandoned and the Zulu army was to disband. Internal and external defence of the realm was to be determined by an appointed group of indunas and British representatives. All Zulu were to be allowed to marry and the kingdom was to allow missionaries to re-establish mission stations and preach unimpeded. In order to ensure adherence to all of the preceding points, a British resident was to be established who, in consultation with Cetshwayo, would hear and judge any dispute which involved a European. No individual could be expelled from the realm without the approval of the British resident. The ultimatum was to expire on 11 January 1879.

Cetshwayo was trapped; he could either contemplate the dismantling of the entire Zulu social and military system, or face war. In any case, the indunas who had listened to the ultimatum were terrified of returning to oNdini to inform the monarch. Although the indunas took some two weeks to report to Cetshwayo, word had already reached him via Dunn. In truth the Zulu had absolutely no conception of the military strength of the British army. They could only measure their military strength in terms of the handful of soldiers which they had seen across the river in Natal. By comparison, the Zulu figured, they had thousands of experienced warriors who could withstand this less than serious threat.

Cetshwayo's inner circle of induna believed that the impending crisis between the British and the Zulu had to be resolved by their king. Indeed Cetshwayo was prepared to turn over Mhlokazulu and to provide the 600 cattle. However, Mhlokazulu commanded part of the iNgobamakhosi and they refused to turn him over.

Dunn was in a difficult position, yet he acted as a means by which messages could be sent between Cetshwayo and the British. He informed them that Cetshwayo would turn over the men and would pay the cattle fines, but that it would take longer than twenty days. The British considered this to be nothing other than evasion and it was determined by Frere that the British army would enter Zululand at the end of the twenty days, but would not launch offensive operations until thirty days had elapsed.

The British army available for any potential invasion was, by any stretch of the imagination, only barely sufficient. It was to be commanded by Lieutenant General Lord Chelmsford (Frederick Augustus Thesinger, the 2nd Baron of Chelmsford). He was a professional soldier, who had seen action in India, Abyssinia and on the Cape frontier against the Xhosa.

When Dunn visited Chelmsford at the Lower Drift around Christmas 1878, it was abundantly clear that the British commander's plans for invasion were well advanced. Dunn had to decide between the British and the Zulu and chose the former; over the next few days he brought 2,000 of his people and around 3,000 cattle out of Zululand and into Natal.

On 4 January 1879 Frere released the following communiqué:

The British forces are crossing into Zululand to exact from Cetywayo [sic] reparation for violations of British territory committed by the sons of Sirayo [sic] and others; and to enforce compliance with the promises, made by Cetywayo [sic] at his coronation, for the better government of his people.

The British Government has no quarrel with the Zulu people. All Zulu who come in unarmed, or who lay down their arms, will be provided for till the troubles of their country are over; and will then, if they please, be allowed to return to their own land; but all who do not so submit will be dealt with as enemies.

On paper, at least, Chelmsford's force, including all ranks, amounted to 16,800 men. But he had decided to create five columns which he proposed would ultimately converge on oNdini. Collectively, however, Chelmsford had access to just six battalions of regular infantry, two artillery batteries and no British cavalry. Even these scant troops would have to be scattered in garrisons along the Natal border. To support the British regulars and, indeed, to make up the bulk of his force, Chelmsford had created three regiments of the Natal Native Contingent (NNC). The strongest of these was the 1 Regiment, which had three battalions, the first having 1,000 men and the other two 2,000 each. As it would transpire these men would prove to be of limited value as only one man in ten was issued with a rifle. They were commanded by local settlers and in many cases men with absolutely no linguistic skills or military experience. For swift movement and manoeuvre, Chelmsford would have to rely upon a patchwork of Colonial units. Some were exclusively white, whilst others were raised from Natal natives who, it must be said, were much better armed and far more reliable than their foot counterparts.

Towards the end of the preparations for invasion Chelmsford reduced the offensive columns from five to three. The centre column, which Chelmsford would accompany, was commanded by Colonel Richard Glyn, and it would cross into Zululand via Rorke's Drift. The south-eastern column (right) was commanded by Colonel Charles Pearson; it would cross into Zululand via the lower Thukela Drift. The third column, under Colonel Henry Evelyn Wood, would cross the Ncome (Blood) River. The two other columns would be placed in reserve, one on the Middle Drift of the Thukela and the other in Transvaal.

It seems that Wood's force moved first, crossing the Ncome on 6 January, where he proceeded to confiscate cattle. Chelmsford and Glyn crossed into Zululand on 11 January and made immediately for Sihayo's kraal which was attacked on 12 January by the 1st Battalion of the 3 Regiment of the NNC, supported by four companies of the 1st Battalion of the 24th. The assaulting force was preceded by all of the cavalry available to the centre column. Initially Glyn had difficulty in forcing the NNC across the difficult terrain towards the kraal. Nonetheless the assault continued, claiming the life of Mkumbikazulu, one of Sihayo's sons who the British had wanted to try in Natal. Sihayo's cattle, sheep and goats were rounded up and his kraal burned down. News of the attack quickly reached Cetshwayo.

Despite the rather inflated figure of 40,000, Cetshwayo had at his disposal no more than 29,000 men; the balance would be needed to maintain order and protect other parts of the kingdom. Strategically Cetshwayo also faced a difficult choice; there were three British columns invading his territory and there was considerable dissention as to how the Zulu army should be deployed. Glyn's attack on Sihayo's kraal settled the matter. The Zulu army would be thrown at the centre column, whilst locally raised troops would deal with the left and right columns. Cetshwayo would send a core of seasoned Zulu troops to stiffen the resistance in these two sectors. In any case, Wood would face Mbilini and the abaQulusi, upon whom the monarch could totally rely. Cetshwayo retained the iNdabakawombe regiment as a personal bodyguard at oNdini. In reality the men, already in their late fifties, would probably add little to the army in the field.

Although the main weight of the Zulu army was dispatched to deal with the centre column, it would be Pearson who would be attacked first. Pearson's troops were not fully into Zululand until 17 January. He had a mixed bag of troops, but at their centre was the 2nd Battalion of the 3 Regiment, the Buffs, which was Pearson's old regiment and the virtually untried and under-strength 99 Regiment. He had just two artillery pieces, a rocket trough, a company of Royal Engineers, a naval detachment from

HMS *Active* and HMS *Tenedos* (with a Gatling gun and two rocket tubes), supported by a squadron of mounted infantry and volunteer cavalry units, including the Natal Hussars and the Victoria, Stanger, Durban and Alexandra Mounted Rifles. Pearson also had two battalions of the 2 Regiment of the NNC and a small contingent known as the Natal Native Pioneer Corps. In total his column amounted to 4,271 men. In order to supply them he had a further 600 wagon drivers and 384 wagons, with just 3,000 oxen.

Pearson had decided that he would advance in two columns, the first, which he called his Flying Column, was to head directly for Eshowe. The second column would be little more than a day behind the first. Pearson's Flying Column began their advance on 18 January. By 21 January Pearson was four miles from the amaTigulu River. Meanwhile Godide kaNdlela was making for kwaGingindlovu. When the Zulu arrived on the afternoon of the 21st, they discovered that a British patrol had already set fire to the kraal. Godide now determined to find Pearson and attack him. Zulu scouts found Pearson encamped, overlooking the Nyezane River. Godide realized that the British were probably fully well aware that he had arrived.

Battle focus

Nyezane

22 January 1879

The British, under Pearson, were underway by 04.30. The column, led by mounted troops, approached the Nyezane River and the mounted men proceeded to scout the heights on the eastern side of the river. The bulk of the troops crossed successfully and began breakfasting on the flat ground, whilst the wagons crossed the drift.

At about 08.00 Zulu scouts appeared on the slopes beside the road which snaked to the north towards Eshowe. Captain Fitzroy Hart was sent in command of a company of the 1st Battalion of the 2 Regiment of Natal Native

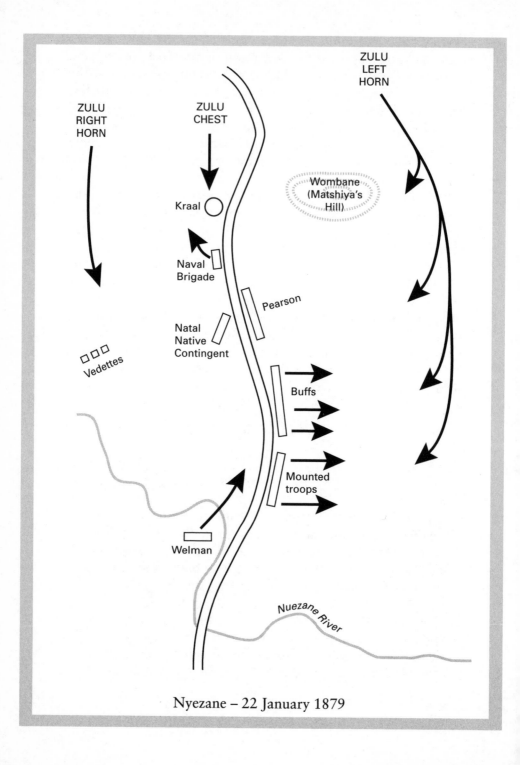

ZULU
RIGHT
HORN

ZULU
CHEST

ZULU
LEFT
HORN

Wombane
(Matshiya's
Hill)

Kraal

Naval
Brigade

Pearson

Natal
Native
Contingent

☐☐☐
Vedettes

Buffs

Mounted
troops

Welman

Nuezane River

Nyezane – 22 January 1879

Contingent (NNC) to probe up the road and clear the Zulu. Hart advanced up the slope of a hill known as Wombane (Matshiya's Hill), to the east of the road. No sooner had they reached the summit than they found themselves facing several hundred Zulu. The NNC fled but the bulk of the officers and NCOs stood and were instantly overrun.

The Zulu commander, Godide kaNdlela, had not intended to precipitate a fight at this juncture and had hoped to catch Pearson's men strung out along the road. Godide was the son of Ndlele kaOmpisi, Dingane's principle induna. He had command of some 3,500 warriors drawn from the uMxapho, the uDlambedlu and the izinGulube regiments. He also had with him elements of local regiments, including the inSukamngeni, the iQwa uDududu and the iNdaba-kawombe. In total his force may have numbered as many as 6,000 men. Godide had three other indunas to assist him; Mbilwane kaMahlanganisa, Masegwane kaSopigwasi and Matshiya.

Ranged against him was Pearson's column which consisted of two 7- pounder guns of No. 11 Battery, 7 Brigade, Royal Artillery, No. 2 Company of the Royal Engineers, five companies of the 2nd Battalion of the Buffs (3 Regiment), two half companies from the 99 Regiment (Duke of Edinburgh's), a naval brigade detachment from HMS *Active,* a detachment of Royal Marine Light Infantry with two 7- pounder guns, a rocket tube and a Gatling gun, No. 2 Squadron of the Mounted Infantry, the Natal Hussars, the Stanger Mounted Rifles, the Victoria Mounted Rifles, both the 1st and 2 Battalions of the 2nd Regiment of the Natal Native Contingent and No. 2 Company of the Natal Native Pioneers. In total Pearson had at his disposal 2,687 men and 95 officers.

The initial Zulu attack was in fact the Zulu left horn, led by the uMxapho regiment. As the firing began the Natal Hussars and the Mounted Infantry spread out facing Wombane. Terrified NNC survivors were streaming down the slope just ahead of the Zulu attack. By the drift both the

101

Victoria and Stanger Rifles remounted and took up position on the opposite side of the road, nearest the river. They deployed along a rise and were able to see the Zulu swarming around the British right and heading for the rear. The Zulu had now approached to within 100 metres of the line thrown up by the Natal Hussars and the Mounted Infantry. More Zulu were swinging around the position of the mounted men. It now became clear that the Zulu were attempting to cut off the lead elements of the British force from the slower moving wagons still crossing the drift.

The line was stiffened by two companies of the Buffs under Jackson and Martin. These companies positioned themselves to the left and right of the Naval Brigade's 7-pounders, just to the east of the road. The guns immediately began firing canisters at the Zulu and a third company of the Buffs arrived to plug the gap in the British line between the Mounted Infantry and the existing Buff companies protecting the Naval Brigade.

In the face of galling musket fire and canisters, the Zulu responded by creeping forward and trading shots with their obsolete muskets. The British fire was increased with the deployment of two x 24-pounder rocket tubes, which, although notoriously inaccurate, terrified the Zulu who had never seen this weapon before. By now the Zulu left horn had approached to within 250 metres of the drift, threatening to work itself around the Mounted Infantry and Natal Hussars. In the nick of time Captain Warren Wynne of the Royal Engineers ordered his men to leave their work at the drift and rush to plug what appeared to be a disastrous gap. Two more companies of the Buffs, under Wyld and Harrison, took up positions to Wynne's right and the Naval Brigade Gatling gun had been brought forward. The Gatling gunfire proved decisive and the left horn was checked.

The battle was not yet over, as the Zulu chest and right horn swarmed towards a kraal just to the west of the road and to the north of the drift. They took up positions around

300 metres from the British left flank. The Zulu were pinned down from effective fire from the Stanger and Victoria Mounted Rifles and no serious attack ever developed. The Zulu abandoned the kraal when well-aimed fire from the rocket tubes set the dry thatch alight.

The British now had the initiative and the Naval Brigade, supported by a company of the Buffs, under Forster and some of Hart's NNC, launched an assault on the burning kraal. Despite the relatively poor shooting of the Zulu, upwards of ten British were either killed or wounded and the assault stalled. Determined to show his sailors' worth, Commander Campbell led his men up the slope and after a vicious mêlée the Zulu began to run. With that the Zulu resolve shattered and they began making off in their hundreds.

By 09.30, just an hour and a half after the first sighting of the Zulu the engagement was over. Between 300 and 400 Zulu had been killed and several hundred wounded. The British had lost twelve killed and had twenty wounded (two of them would subsequently die).

After two hours Pearson pressed on, eager to prove that the Zulu attack had no bearing on his plans.

Despite having beaten the Zulu, Pearson was to discover as late as 26 January that a disaster had befallen the centre column, which would now put his position in grave jeopardy. He was un-supported and there was every chance that the full weight of the Zulu army would now fall on him. Pearson took up position at Eshowe and the Zulu encircled him and effectively put him under siege for the next three months.

The terrain through which Chelmsford and the centre column would have to traverse was wholly unsuitable for oxen and wagons. He would have to cross the Batshe Valley and then the Manzimnyama stream. The route then passed Isandlwana, before he could cross a plain and make for oNdini. Chelmsford began crossing Rorke's Drift on 20 January and proposed to set up his next camp at Isandlwana. The hill, being an isolated part of the iNyoni, rose some 300 feet. Bizarrely the rock formation closely resembled the sphinx on the badge of the 24 Regiment. The site was a good one, if a little rocky, and fresh water was close by.

Chelmsford had gone to great lengths to explain to his column commanders prior to the invasion that any camp should be laagered and preferably entrenched, yet he chose to ignore his own advice. Chelmsford seems to have been perfectly well aware that at least a significant element of the Zulu army was on its way towards him, having left oNdini some three days before. Chelmsford figured that the Isandlwana campsite provided an ideal vantage point from which he could see across the plain and he was, in fact, only thirty miles from Colonel Wood's column. He took the prudent step to begin scouting ahead to find the Zulu army. He dispatched Major John Dartnell and his Natal Mounted Police, with the assistance of the 3 Regiment of the NNC, to leave Isandlwana at first light on 21 January. Dartnell's men were to search as far as the Mangeni gorge. The NNC rendezvoused with Dartnell at the Mangeni gorge towards the end of the afternoon. Dartnell then headed off in the direction of oNdini, where he encountered a large number of Zulu; they had swiftly disappeared into the landscape. Dartnell was faced with a difficult decision; he could leave now for Isandlwana and make it back before nightfall, but the intelligence he would be able to give to Chelmsford would be incomplete. He therefore decided to order the NNC to take up a position at the end of the Hlazakazi Ridge, while he would investigate the Mangeni gorge.

No sooner had Dartnell's men covered 200 or 300 metre than they saw another large body of Zulu. The Zulu retired, but Dartnell decided not to give chase as he believed that they were trying to lure him into an ambush. Dartnell still did not know whether a large Zulu force was in the region and he sent back a message to Chelmsford, which arrived at Isandlwana at 01.30. Chelmsford determined to march out and rendezvous with Dartnell, believing this to be the lead elements of the Zulu army.

Battle focus

Isandlwana

22 January 1879

Isandlwana is, perhaps, the most misunderstood and misrepresented battle of the Anglo-Zulu War.

Chelmsford had begun leaving the base camp at around 02.30 that morning. He had left behind five companies of the 1st Battalion of the 24th, one company of the 2nd Battalion of the 24th, 130 mounted troops, two Royal Artillery pieces and a sizeable number of the 3 Regiment of the Natal Native Contingent (NNC). The camp, unfortified and unlaagered, was under the command of Colonel Henry Pulleine (1st Battalion, 24 Regiment). Before leaving, Chelmsford had sent a message to Brevet Colonel Anthony Durnford, who commanded a detachment of No. 2 column, which had recently moved from the middle drift to Rorke's Drift. Durnford was to move up to Isandlwana.

The British spotted a large number of Zulu on the iNyoni Ridge at around 06.00; this was to the left of the camp. Pulleine mustered his regular companies and sent scouts onto the ridge, who reported that the Zulu were retiring to the north-east. The men were still standing-to at 10.30, when Durnford rode into the camp at the head of his Natal Native Horse, comprising three troops of Sikalis' horse. With him he had two Royal Artillery rocket troughs, under Major Russell, and the 1 Regiment of the NNC.

Durnford was apprised of the situation and at this point there is the first level of confusion with regard to the battle and the way in which it was conducted. Technically, Durnford outranked Pulleine and it is not clear whether Chelmsford expected Durnford to command at Isandlwana or not. Beyond being called up to Isandlwana, Durnford had no further orders. It must be assumed that as Pulleine was an experienced officer, who had fought during the Cape

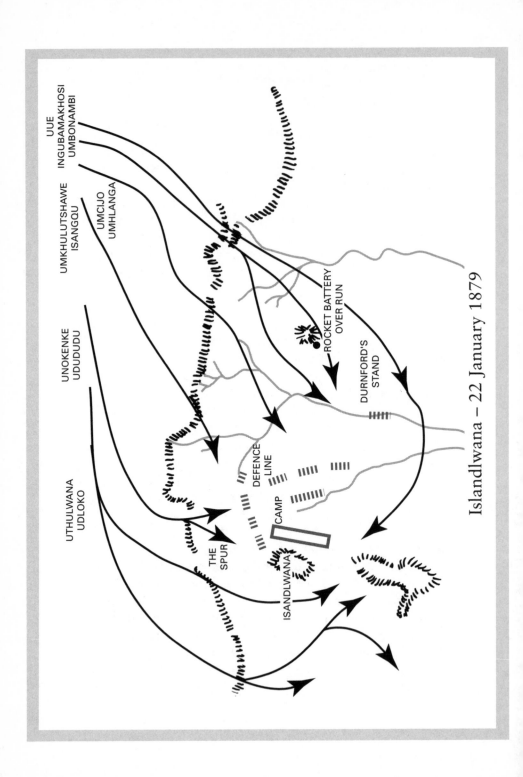

UUE
INGUBAMAKHOSI
UMBONAMBI

UMKHULUTSHAWE
ISANGQU

UMCIJO
UMHLANGA

UNOKENKE
UDUDUDU

UTHULWANA
UDLOKO

ROCKET BATTERY
OVER RUN

DURNFORD'S
STAND

DEFENCE
LINE

CAMP

THE
SPUR

ISANDLWANA

Islandlwana – 22 January 1879

Frontier War, he was perfectly capable of making his own decisions based on the very simple instructions to defend the camp. Be that as it may, Durnford was somewhat impetuous and was concerned that the presence of the Zulu on the iNyoni Ridge meant that there was an enemy force behind Chelmsford, who was already well on the way to the Mangeni Gorge. Durnford decided that he would lead his troops out of the camp and deal with any Zulu he encountered and ensure that they were not harassing Chelmsford's line of communication. His only suggestion and request to Pulleine was that as the Zulu had withdrawn, there was no need for the regular companies to still be on the alert and that if Durnford ran into difficulties, he would hope that Pulleine would send him assistance.

Durnford rode out of the camp at around 11.30, before his supply wagons had arrived. Durnford sent two troops of the Natal Native Horse (under Raw and Roberts) onto a ridge to the north of the camp. It was supported by Cavaye's company of the 24th. Durnford took the rest of his mounted men across the plain to the east, with the intention of flushing out the Zulu in the immediate area.

Raw and Roberts had ridden some three or four miles when they saw some Udibi boys with several head of cattle. They decided to give chase. By the time they closed with them they had reached the Ngwebeni Valley and below them, to their absolute horror, were upwards of 24,000 Zulu.

It now appeared that Chelmsford was on a wild goose chase. The Zulu army had not been making its way south-west, but north-west. Major John Dartnell, who had been sent out to patrol by Chelmsford, had in fact encountered Matshana kaMondise's warriors who were heading to join the main Zulu army. It was these men who Chelmsford was now marching to deal with, believing them to be the main Zulu force.

The Zulu, commanded by Ntshingwayo kaMahole and Mavumengwana kaNdlela, had not intended to attack the British until the following day (as a result of the new moon and the 22nd not being a significant lunar date). Nonetheless, as soon as the mounted men appeared above them, there was no option but to attack. The first Zulu to spring into action were the uKhandempemvu, who immediately began to charge towards Raw's men, who replied with a volley. They then fell back on Robert's troop. Unsurprisingly, the two troops then made straight for the camp.

The bulk of the Zulu army was now on its feet and surging out of the Ngwebeni Valley. The two induna managed to hold back the uThulwana, iNdlondlo, uDloko and the iNdluyengwe (known as the oNdini corps). These men were the only ones to have the pre-battle ritual and would operate as reserves in the forthcoming battle.

As the Zulu army ran from the Ngwebeni Valley to the INyoni Ridge, some kind of order was re-established. The chest comprised the uMbonambi, the uKhandempemvu and the uNokhenke. The right horn was formed from the iMbube, the iSangqu and the uDududu. The younger regiments took up position as the left horn, namely the uVe and the iNgobamakhosi.

As Raw and Roberts fled towards the camp, a messenger was sent to warn them, but as the iNyoni Ridge blocked the view, Pulleine simply believed that the messenger was exaggerating. He still did not believe that the Zulu army could be anywhere near the camp. Nonetheless, he sent a second company, under Mostyn, to support Cavaye's company. No sooner had Mostyn's company disappeared beyond the ridge, than the camp could hear heavy firing from that direction.

A second messenger from Raw reached Durnford, who was on an escarpment and was about to turn to his northeast. He was some miles from the camp and had brought with him the rocket battery and an escort of NNC. These had lagged behind his mounted troops. Suddenly, the leading elements of the iNgobamakhosi and the uVe came into view. Durnford immediately ordered his troops to dismount and volley the rapidly approaching Zulu left horn. With laudable precision, Durnford's men fired a volley, retreated 100 metres, dismounted and fired once more across the plain, with the Zulu now little more than fifty metres from them.

The rocket battery and its escort had reached a conical koppie to the south of the escarpment. Russell spotted what he believed to be an isolated group of Zulu and deployed his tubes. They managed to get one shot off before the iNgobamakhosi overran them. Russell was killed, as was most of the crew. However, one officer and some NNC withstood the attack and were picked up by Durnford's mounted troops on their retreat towards the camp.

Pulleine now deployed Major Smith's artillery to support Mostyn and Cavaye. The artillery took up a commanding position covering the iNyoni Ridge. Two more companies of the 1st Battalion of the 24th (Wardell and Porteous) were deployed either side of the artillery. Pulleine could still see no Zulu, but he firmly believed that any attack would come from the north. He now deployed a company of the NNC and his only company of the 2nd Battalion, 24th (under Pope) to take up position on the far right of the British line. Collectively, the British could now theoretically at least deny any possible attack emanating from the north.

In a few moments the lead elements of the Zulu chest began coming over the ridge. Pulleine dispatched Lieutenant Melvill, his adjutant, to call Mostyn and Cavaye back and fall into line for fear that they would be overrun. Younghusband's company of the 1st Battalion was sent to cover the withdrawal. With some confusion Mostyn, Cavaye, Raw and Roberts all fell back and into line, anchoring the position alongside Porteous. The lead Zulu regiment, the uNokhenke, was severely punished with well aimed volleys and artillery fire and fell back beyond the ridge.

Meanwhile, Durnford's mounted troops had fallen back to a donga known as Nyogane. It was already occupied by a small, mounted patrol sent out from the camp. Durnford and his men took up position along the donga, barely 1,000 metres from the camp. The Zulu left horn was close behind them, but there was some fifty metres of open ground for the Zulu to cross and Durnford's men fired volley after volley into them. Both the uVe and the iNgobamakhosi were halted dead in their tracks. It seemed for a moment that the Zulu had been stopped, but there was a vast gap of several hundred metres between Durnford and Pope, who held the far right of the British line. Into this gap flowed the uMbonambi. For several crucial minutes Durnford, supported by Pope's fire, prevented the Zulu from surging through the gap. On Durnford's right, however, he was in grave danger of being outflanked. Elements of the iNgobamakhosi, in an attempt to avoid the galling fire, were working round Durnford's right.

There was another, more pressing problem; Durnford's men were running short of ammunition. Riders were sent for resupply, but with Durnford's own supplies not yet up from Rorke's Drift, the 24th's quartermasters refused to give Durnford's Natal Native Horse ammunition.

It was now shortly after 13.00 and Durnford, realizing that he was in an exposed position with little ammunition, decided to abandon the donga. At the same time Pope chose to move to his right to support Durnford. Only a single, regular company was now ranged against the entire Zulu left horn. No sooner had this move taken place than Pulleine ordered his bugler to sound the withdrawal. He intended that his companies should fall back on the camp, providing a more compact defensive position.

The Zulu commanders were now intent on closing with the British, despite not having planned the battle. An induna was sent to the uKhandempemvu to goad them into action. They began to spring forward and this heartened the iNgobamakhosi, who could see their rival regiment taking the initiative.

The British withdrawal was somewhat confused, with the Natal Native Horse and the NNC retiring somewhat faster than the regular British companies. In a matter of seconds the Zulu took advantage of the situation and were amongst

110

the British. Smith's artillery barely managed to get away. The uKhandempemvu was at the brunt of the fighting, forcing the British south as they were in hand-to-hand fighting with Mostyn, Cavaye and Younghusband's men. They were also engaged to the north-east with Wardell and Porteous. Meanwhile, Pope was being attacked by the uMbonambi.

While the Zulu cut through the disintegrating British line and flooded in among the camp's tents, slaughtering anything that moved, Durnford ordered his mounted Natives to abandon the battlefield and took up position himself along the track through the camp, with a group of Natal settlers. Bizarrely, just before 14.00 there was a solar eclipse, but the darkness failed to even temporarily interrupt the hand-to-hand combat.

Small knots of the British force began to fall back, sorely pressed towards the Manzimnyama Valley, only to discover that the escape route towards Rorke's Drift had been cut by the Zulu right horn. The uDududu, the iSangqu, the iMbube and the majority of the uNokhenke were pouring into the camp from the rear. Durnford and his small group of men desperately tried to hold back the iNgobamakhosi on the track, but they were overwhelmed by sheer weight of numbers.

In the centre of the camp, elements of several regular companies attempted to make a last stand, and for a short while the Zulu were held off by concentrated fire, but once again thrown spears and concerted charges by the Zulu overwhelmed the British. Only Younghusband's company, which had been on the far left of the British line still had any degree of cohesion. They retreated towards Isandlwana itself and took up positions on the slope. Another group of British regulars was slowly retreating, firing as it went, towards the Manzimnyama Valley. The terrain was very difficult and it appears that it reached the bank of the stream but was then overrun.

The unequal struggle continued for upwards of an hour. At least one British regular, possibly a survivor from

111

Younghusband's company, which had run out of ammunition and was overwhelmed, hid in a cave and sniped at the Zulu until he was killed some hours later.

Sometime towards the end of the British resistance Lieutenant Teignmouth Melvill (1st Battalion of the 24th's adjutant), snatched up the Queen's colour and attempted to bring it safely off the battlefield. He linked up with Lieutenant Neville Coghill and they managed to make it to the Mzinyathi River. They jumped in on their horses. Coghill made it across but Melvill lost his horse and the strong current pulled him downstream. Coghill turned back and with the aid of a NNC officer, Higginson, pulled Melvill out of the water. Some Zulu had already crossed into Natal and Higginson made off to find horses. Melvill and Coghill were tracked down by the Zulu and killed. It appears that both banks of the river were swarming with Zulu. Indeed the oNdini (Ulundi) corps had swept through this area and had only managed to kill a handful of running men that had not taken part in the battle itself.

Cetshwayo had given explicit instructions that the army would not violate Natal's territory. Their commander, Dabulamanzi kaMpande, was determined to gain some glory for his regiments and advanced along the river towards Rorke's Drift.

Meanwhile, back in the camp, the vast majority of the British force was already dead and the Zulu began looting the camp. Aside from taking around 1,000 Martini-Henry rifles and several hundred thousand rounds of ammunition, they took anything else of any remote value, including the red jackets of the fallen 24th. There had been some 1,700 men in the camp, including the elements of Durnford's column, at the time of the attack. Not a single member of the six companies of the 24th survived. In all, fifty-two officers, 806 white other ranks and 500 native allies had been slaughtered. Just sixty whites and around 400 natives had managed to escape.

The Zulu had lost around 1,000 men killed during the

battle and a similar number had been badly wounded. They had spared nothing in the camp and the majority of the 3,000 oxen had been slaughtered, together with officer and artillery horses and mules and even pet dogs. By dusk the bulk of the Zulu army had returned to the Ngwebeni Valley, having placed shields over their fallen and dragged other Zulu dead into dongas, where they were covered with stones. All of the British fallen had been ritually dis-embowelled in line with Zulu beliefs and tradition. The Zulu army eventually made its weary way back to report to Cetshwayo at oNdini (Ulundi).

In direct contravention to Cetshwayo's orders Dabulamanzi kaMpande led his oNdini (Ulundi) corps across the Mzinyathi River towards Rorke's Drift. The supply depot was based around the buildings which had been constructed first by James Rorke and then added to by Otto Witt, the Swedish missionary. Witt's chapel had been converted into a store run by Assistant Commissary, Walter Dunn, Acting Assistant Commissary, James Dalton and their storekeeper, Louis Byrne. Witt's home had been converted into a hospital, housing Surgeon Reynolds and three of his men who were looking after thirty-five sick or injured men. Technically at least, the supply depot was commanded by Major Spalding, but he had left his post in the morning to ride to Helpmekaar to enquire why a reinforcing company of the 24th had not arrived. He left the post under the command of Lieutenant John Chard (Royal Engineers), but the main force at the post was B Company of the 2nd Battalion, 24th (some eighty men) commanded by Lieutenant Gonville Bromhead.

Towards the end of the morning of the 22nd the post had heard firing and shortly after, two mounted officers of the Natal Native Contingent (NNC) gave Chard and Bromhead the terrible news that the camp at Isandlwana had been overrun. Reynolds and Chaplain George Smith climbed up the Oskarberg (Shiyane Hill) to see if they could detect any movement. They could clearly see fighting along the banks of the Manzimnyana. It was quickly decided that to abandon the post would be the worst possible option as the Zulu would undoubtedly catch up with the garrison, as they would need to load the sick onto wagons.

Battle focus

Rorke's Drift

22-23 January 1879

Chard and Bromhead, in consultation with Dalton, (who had been a Quartermaster Sergeant) decided to use the enormous supply of biscuit boxes and sacks of mealies in order to create a defensive position around the main buildings. Together with a detachment of Natal Native Contingent (NNC) under Stephenson, a barricade was created linking the two buildings. Wagons were pushed into place for further defence.

No sooner had the defence works been completed than a group of Natal Native Horse, led by a white officer, arrived and Chard ordered them to form a screen to the south of the Oskarberg. By now Smith and Reynolds had returned and confirmed that they had seen enormous numbers of Zulu heading towards Rorke's Drift.

At 16.30 the lead elements of the Zulu force appeared (probably 500-600 men). The Natal Native Horse promptly bolted, followed by Stephenson's NNC. Chard, Bromhead and Dalton now had just eight officers and 131 men, including the sick and injured. It was quickly decided to run a second line of barricades, connecting the storehouse to the existing barricade. The British could now see the full weight of the Zulu force, some 4,000 men.

The Zulu attacked in close formation, heading towards the rear of the British position. The British began firing at around 400 metres, but the Zulu continued their headlong rush. They got to within forty-five metres or so before the additional fire from the buildings and wagons stopped them and they went to ground around a drainage ditch and the abandoned British cookhouse. Many of the Zulu lapped

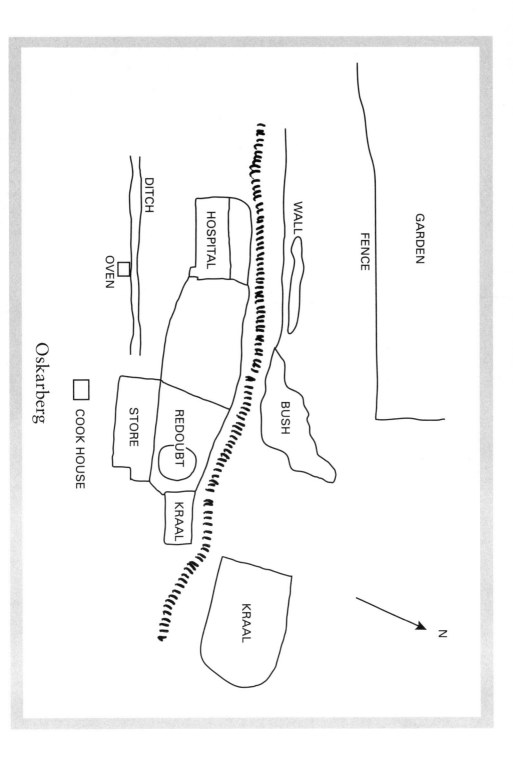

Oskarberg

☐ COOK HOUSE

GARDEN

FENCE

WALL

BUSH

DITCH

OVEN

HOSPITAL

STORE

REDOUBT

KRAAL

KRAAL

N

around the British position, heading for the hospital. This was the weak point in the line and the Zulu were able to drive the British away from the front of the hospital. Here they began to attempt to break into the building.

While all this was taking place, a large group of Zulu had taken up position on the Oskarberg and were beginning to pour fire down into the British position. Luckily for the British, the Zulu had somewhat antiquated weapons and in terms of accuracy and range they were no match for the Martini-Henry. Nonetheless the Zulu did score some hits on the defenders.

Back at the hospital, the Zulu had broken into the building. As luck would have it, Rorke had constructed the building in a very odd manner in as much as each of the rooms was not connected. This allowed the defenders to hold each room for just long enough for the majority of the men to retreat to the next room before the Zulu overran them one at a time. There was desperate fighting inside the building and an even more desperate race for the defenders to break through the wall into the next room before the Zulu gained access. Ultimately the British were driven out of the building and to add to the confusion the hospital was now on fire. The British had now fallen back to the area around the storehouse and the majority of the patients had been dragged into the new British position.

The Zulu attacked towards the cattle kraal to the east of the storehouse. Again the British were driven back towards a redoubt which had been constructed. The British were confined to a very compact area and for the majority of the night they had to withstand innumerable assaults.

Daylight finally came and the area around the redoubt was littered with Zulu dead, but the Zulu army had withdrawn. The British sent out patrols and collected up the discarded Zulu weapons. Suddenly the Zulu army returned, but this time they paused out of rifle range then gradually retreated. They could see what the British could not see; Chelmsford's force was approaching Rorke's Drift from the devastation of the Isandlwana battlefield.

Some 370 Zulu had been killed in the immediate vicinity of Rorke's Drift. The British had suffered fifteen deaths (two more had mortal wounds) and many of the others were wounded.

Whilst the battles at Isandlwana and Rorke's Drift raged, Chelmsford had spent an unproductive day casting around for Zulu amongst the hills surrounding the Mangeni gorge. Chelmsford had sent his contingent of NNC back towards the camp in the late morning of the 22nd. It was they who saw the Zulu left horn heading towards Isandlwana. By the time he could respond to the news and gather up his troops, which were scattered over a considerable area, the battle was already lost. He did not return to the camp until the late afternoon, by which time darkness had fallen. His men were exhausted, having marched some twenty-four miles to and from the Mangeni gorge. They then had to spend a fitful night alongside the dead left in the wake of the Zulu attack; they could even see flames in the sky which alerted them to the fact that Rorke's Drift had been attacked.

Chelmsford roused his troops shortly before dawn and headed back towards Rorke's Drift. They encountered large groups of Zulu retreating from the failed assault on the little mission station. Scouts reached Rorke's Drift first and sent word that the garrison had not been massacred. However none of the troops, which Chelmsford had hoped had escaped from Isandlwana, was present. Chelmsford had no option but to retire and begin organizing defences in Natal for what seemed like the inevitable Zulu invasion.

Of the three columns which had entered Zululand, Glyn's had been severely mauled, Pearson was besieged at Eshowe and only Wood was still capable of striking against the Zulu. Meanwhile, the Zulu who had fought at Isandlwana needed to go through their purification ceremonies; above all rest was needed and mourning for the dead. The Zulu had won at great cost; the first clashes of the Anglo-Zulu War had taken place.

Chapter Eight

Cetshwayo kaMpande
March–August 1879

Pearson received confirmation of the centre column's demise on 28 January. He faced the stark choice of either retiring or digging in. Instead he decided on a compromise and sent his Natal Volunteers and the Natal Native Contingent (NNC) back across the Thukela, while the balance of his force dug in. There were considerable numbers of Zulu in the immediate vicinity and on 29 January they managed to sweep in and take away 900 head of cattle. Nonetheless they did not choose to close on Pearson's position, probably as a result of the instructions Cetshwayo had already given them. Pearson's defence force, now ensconced in Fort Eshowe, consisted of some 1,339 white officers and men and 355 black Natal Volunteers. The Zulu, it appears, had decided that rather than assault Pearson's fort, they would starve him out by attacking any relief column on its way to assist him.

Pearson was not content with simply sitting and waiting and on 1 March he sent a column to destroy a kraal seven miles from the fort. It caught the Zulu by surprise and the column was able to destroy the kraal and retire in good order to the fort, despite the Zulu's best attempts to surround them. There was continual sniping from Zulu hidden in the grass and cover around the fort which caused a number of casualties.

As early as the middle of February, Pearson had been informed by a messenger that Chelmsford was organizing a relief column, but March dawned with still no sign of assistance. Before Chelmsford was ready to move there was to be another disaster, although mercifully not of the proportions that had befallen the British at Isandlwana. Notably the setback was caused by none other than Mbilini.

Colonel Wood and his column, consisting of two infantry battalions (1st Battalion, 13th Light Infantry and the 90th Light Infantry), supported by four 7-pounders and two rocket troughs, six troops of mounted volunteers and Wood's irregulars (two battalions of local Zulu) was intended to support Chelmsford's centre column. Wood's column would have to traverse the disputed land between Transvaal and Zululand. His main base was Utrecht and his forward base was Luneburg. Supplies would have to move up from Utrecht, through Luneburg and ultimately to Derby. This was where Colonel Hugh Rowlands and his column were positioned. Rowlands had the 80 Regiment, some Swazi allies and a number of mounted volunteers. Rowlands had already established a garrison at Luneburg.

It was clear to both Wood and to Cetshwayo that Luneburg was a strategically important position. It was only fifty miles to the north of Hlobane and was also within striking distance, particularly based around the Ntombe Valley, of two aggressive tribes, one led by Manyanyoba kaMaqondo and the other by Mbilini kaMswati. Both men would deploy their forces, as well as the abaQulusi, against Wood.

Wood had established his headquarters in Zululand, at Fort Tinta. Lieutenant Colonel Redvers Buller, acting under Wood, mounted a series of patrols as far as the Zungwini Mountain; this was very close to the abaQulusi stronghold at Hlobane. Despite the growing Zulu concentration in the area, Wood did not commit his troops to anything other than a series of small skirmishes.

A notable development occurred on 10 March, when Hamu came over to the British at Wood's new base of operations at Khambula, which was positioned closer to Luneburg and the Ntombe Valley, as well as barring the way between Hlobane and Utrecht. Wood's column had been reinforced by mounted infantry under Russell, the Edendale Contingent of the Natal Native Horse, Raaf's Transvaal Rangers and the Border Horse. Rowlands' command was also placed directly under the control of Wood and all except a small detachment, the 80th, marched to Khambula. The rest were left at Luneburg, under Major Charles Tucker. Columns of wagons carrying ammunition and supplies were constantly en route from Rowlands' former headquarters at Derby.

It was one such column, held up by torrential rain, that was to be the direct cause of the next British reversal on the Ntombe River.

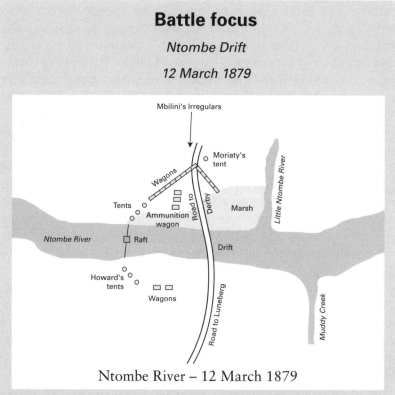

Battle focus

Ntombe Drift

12 March 1879

Ntombe River – 12 March 1879

The battle at Ntombe Drift is far lesser known than the disaster at Isandlwana. This may be as the result of the scale of the defeat, but more importantly its relatively low strategic significance.

The Zulu force, in fact largely made up of allied Swazi, was led by Mbilini. There have been various estimates as to the number of men he had available to him, ranging as high as 4,000, but the exact strength was probably closer to 800.

On 7 March Major Charles Tucker, in command of five companies of the Staffordshire Volunteers (80 Regiment) based at Luneburg, sent Captain David Moriarty to bring in an overdue supply column of eighteen wagons, which was en route to Luneburg from Derby. Moriarty had 106 officers and men at his command and by 9 March he had gathered together the wagons and had crossed to the north bank of the Ntombe River. The torrential rain had prevented him from moving two of the wagons, which were still on the southern bank. Moriarty had no option but to wait until the level of the river dropped. Major Tucker visited him and warned Moriarty that he should laager the wagons. Consequently Moriarty positioned the wagons in a v-shape, facing away from the river. But the wagons were not lashed together and when the river began to drop a considerable gap was left between the last wagons and the river bank.

Moriarty had positioned seventy-one of his men on the northern bank and his remaining thirty-four men, under the command of Lieutenant H. H. Harward and Sergeant Anthony Booth, were on the south bank. Communication between the two commands was possible by shouting across the river, but also via a raft.

At approximately 03.30 on 12 March a single shot was heard. Harward requested orders from Moriarty, but was told that there was nothing to be concerned about and that his men should go back to sleep. As it was, Mbilini's stronghold (Tafelberg) was barely five kilometres from Moriarty's position and it is said that Mbilini himself was among a group of Zulu who had visited the laager on 11 March.

An hour and a half later a sentry on the southern bank spotted a group of Zulu creeping towards Moriarty's laager. They approached to within around sixty-five metres, fired a volley into the tents and then rushed the camp. No sooner had the infantry struggled out of their tents than the Zulu were upon them. Moriarty is said to have shot several

Zulu, despite having been speared before he, too, was finally shot. The bulk of Moriarty's men were slaughtered where they stood or lay. A scant few plunged into the river and made for the south bank; they were swiftly followed by upwards of 200 Zulu.

Harward's men took up position near their two wagons, directed by Booth. Harward jumped on his horse and shouted to Booth that he was riding for Luneburg to bring help. Meanwhile Booth managed to collect together Corporal Burgess and seven other ranks and in the chaos slowly retreated five kilometres south, taking up a position in a deserted farmhouse.

The Zulu pursued for a while and then fell back to the drift to loot the laager and deal with any British stragglers. The net result of the brief action accounted for sixty-two members of the company, along with seventeen civil wagon drivers. It is unclear exactly how many of Mbilini's men were killed; certainly British claims of 200 are grossly exaggerated. Harward had reached Luneburg at 06.30 and accompanied by Major Tucker and 150 mounted men, they rode to the drift. A single survivor of the 80th and a wagon driver were overjoyed to see them. In the immediate vicinity only thirty Zulu corpses were found.

Harward was sentenced to be court-martialled for desertion, but he was found not guilty. In order to prove a point, however, details of his conduct were read to each regiment in the British army. Booth, who had shown considerable presence of mind, was promoted to Colour Sergeant and awarded the Victoria Cross.

Whilst the action at Ntombe had been something of a setback, elsewhere Chelmsford's troops were recovering. Fresh reinforcements were making their way up from Durban and Chelmsford's first major task was to deal with the situation at Eshowe.

Cetshwayo was concerned with Hamu's defection. Wood's troops were also a concern, as was the fact that Pearson's force was still in Zulu territory. Nonetheless Cetshwayo sent messengers to talk peace with Chelmsford. It seems that Cetshwayo genuinely believed that a peaceful solution could be reached, but this was not Chelmsford's intention. At the very least he wanted revenge for Isandlwana.

Wood represented the biggest threat and Mbilini's troops, along with Manyanyoba and the abaQulusi were all that was preventing Wood from making progress. Cetshwayo therefore dispatched his main army, after two months of rest, to assist Mbilini. Cetshwayo had learned lessons from previous encounters and positively forbade the army to attack the British if they were in a laagered position.

Chelmsford was already well advanced and was gathering his forces at Fort Pearson on the lower drift, in order to relieve Eshowe. He ordered a number of diversionary raids across the Thukela and Mzingathi Rivers, but his main target was the abaQuluzi's strong point at Hlobane.

Hlobane (eHlobane) would be a tough nut to crack. The mountain consisted of three main promontories, running south-west to north-east, encompassing Ntendeka, Hlobane and Ityenka. The most promising approach was the connection between Hlobane and Ityenka, but the pass which connected Ntendeka to Hlobane was very steep. In any case, patrols had reported that the tracks were blocked by stone walls. There were two other reasons why Hlobane proved to be an irresistible target. First there were rumours that Mbilini was in the process of organizing his own offensive, but more importantly the seizure of the abaQulusi's cattle would be welcomed by the Boer irregulars and impress Hamu.

Battle focus

Hlobane (eHlobane)

28 March 1879

Colonel Henry Evelyn Wood's column would be split into two distinct groups. The first was commanded by Lieutenant Colonel J. C. Russell. In effect Russell's column

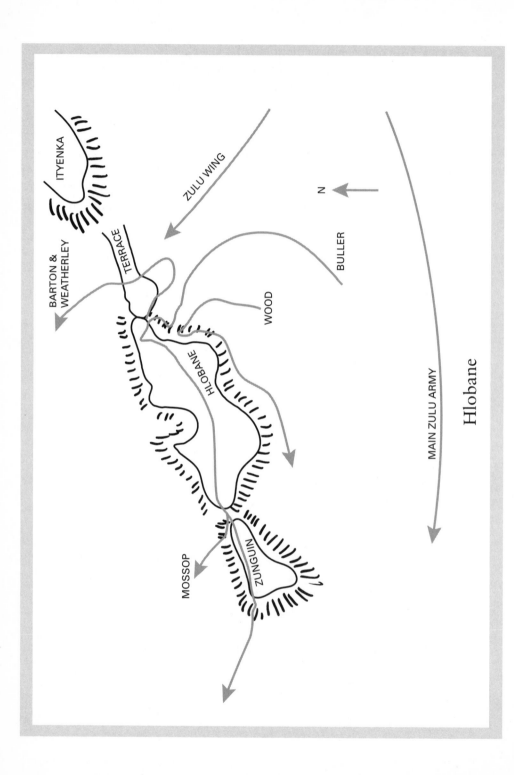

ITYENKA

ZULU WING

N

BULLER

BARTON &
WEATHERLEY

TERRACE

WOOD

HLOBANE

MAIN ZULU ARMY

MOSSOP

ZUNGUIN

Hlobane

would play a subsidiary role to the slightly larger force commanded by Brevet Lieutenant Colonel Redvers Buller. Russell's force of 640 men included No. 11 Battery, 7 Brigade of the Royal Artillery, with their rockets, mounted infantry, the Mounted Kaffarian Rifles, elements of the Natal Native force and the 1st Battalion of Wood's Irregulars, coupled with warriors belonging to Hamu. Buller's command amount to 675 officers and men. He, too, had a rocket party of No. 11 Battery, 7 Brigade Royal Artillery, around 160 Frontier Light Horse and upwards of 200 irregular cavalry drawn from the Transvaal Rangers, the Border Horse and Boers under the command of Piet Uys. In addition to this Buller also had 280 men from the 2nd Battalion of Wood's irregulars. Buller's task was to approach Hlobane via the connection between Hlobane and Ityenka.

Both groups began their approach at around 03.30 on 28 March. Although they had probably been spotted having camped four miles from Hlobane for the night, a thunderstorm with accompanying lightning no doubt assisted the abaQulusi to see them. They had certainly reached the track leading up into Hlobane at 06.30, when they came under fire. Several members of the Frontier Light Horse were hit. Uys' Boers spurred themselves forward and managed to break up the Zulu resistance. Unbeknown to Buller, a group of abaQulusi warriors had slipped behind him and cut off his chance of a retreat. Meanwhile Buller contented himself with rounding up the abundant cattle at the top of the mountain.

Meanwhile Wood had begun his approach towards Ntendeka, but had discovered that the pass was impossible for horses. He sent a group of his mounted infantry up on foot in order to link up with Buller. Wood and a small escort now worked around the south-eastern edge of Hlobane, attempting to link up with the track Buller had taken to the summit. It was here he found Colonel Weatherley and his Border Horse. They had been separated from Buller in the darkness and ominously had found it impossible to follow

Buller due to the abaQulusi, who had cut the track behind Buller. Even now Wood and Weatherley were under heavy fire. Wood led the way, with the Border Horse following him. They came under tremendous fire from the Zulu; several officers were hit and Wood's horse was killed. The Border Horse seemed reluctant to winkle the Zulu out. The abaQulusi were barely thirty metres away, but Wood was insistent that the officers should be buried where they had fallen.

Buller, meanwhile, had collected the bulk of the abaQulusi cattle, but the rearguard he had positioned to cover the track was under heavy fire from increasing numbers of Zulu. Suddenly a large number of Zulu emerged from Ityenka and were hastening towards the mountain's connection with Hlobane. Buller desperately tried to drive the cattle back down the track towards Russell's command, which had scaled Ntendeka. By now Buller's rearguard was in danger of being overrun.

It now appears that a confusing order was issued by Buller. He told a troop of the Frontier Light Horse, commanded by Captain Barton, to retire by the right of the mountain. Barton interpreted the order as best he could and immediately found Weatherley's Border Horse. They both interpreted Buller's instructions to retire as best they could, which they promptly did, causing additional chaos for Buller, as they headed north-east then north, away from the mountain.

Russell, on the top of Ntendeka, could see, to his horror, the main Zulu army approaching Hlobane from the direction of oNdini (Ulundi). He quickly wrote a note to Wood to warn him, instructing him to retreat towards Ntendeka. This was all taking place amidst the chaos of several hundred cattle and sheep being driven towards Russell.

Wood had already seen the danger, as would Mtonga, Cetshwayo's half-brother, who had fled to the Transvaal and was leading his followers. Buller, it appears, was the last to realize the imminent danger. He quickly figured that there would be no possibility of a retreat to the south, back down the track which he had taken to the summit. Equally, he realized that Barton had misinterpreted his orders. He had meant to tell Barton to head west, towards Ntendeka and he attempted to recall him. Meanwhile he ordered his own command to link up with Russell.

The lead element of the Zulu army was, in fact, the right horn, amongst which were the uKhandempemvu, the iNgobamakhosi and the uVe. The Zulu army had not expected to be rushing straight into battle, but as they came over the Inyathi Hills they could see fighting in the distance and hastened to join in. The right horn quickly approached Hlobane. The uKhandempemvu headed for the connection between Hlobane and Ityenka, while the other two regiments swung towards Ntendeka.

To Barton's and Weatherley's dismay, they had come down the eastern end of the mountain range and were beginning to head off south just as the lead elements of the uKhandempemvu hove into view. They were now in a desperate situation; they could not escape to the south and their retreat back up the pass between Hlobane and Ityenka was now blocked by the abaQulusi. In retrospect they probably chose the right option and headed back up the pass, but by now it was swarming with Zulu and behind them the uKhandempemvu was closing fast. The vast majority of Weatherley's and Barton's commands were caught and killed, including the two commanders. It is said that Barton was killed by Sitshitshili kaMnquandi (an uKhandempemvu induna) after a considerable chase along the mountain. A few of Barton's and Weatherley's command managed to extricate themselves.

Meanwhile, back at the top of the summit, Buller's rearguard had disintegrated and what remained was being hunted down by the abaQulusi. It was now every man for himself as Buller's tattered command reached the pass at the western edge of Hlobane, which led down to Ntendeka. It was a perilous route, quite rightly named the Devil's Pass.

A desperate rearguard attempted to hold the abaQulusi back but this was soon overwhelmed and, with the abaQulusi firing into them with both muskets and spears and even boulders, the casualties were mounting fast. Somehow Piet Uys had been unhorsed and he was speared in the descent. By now what remained of Buller's command was at the bottom of the pass. Another rearguard was quickly formed, but it was now being harassed by the lead elements of the iNgobamakhosi, who were tearing up the southern slope of Ntendeka.

Wood and Russell had already begun their retreat to the south of Zungwini Mountain, managing to withdraw relatively intact. Wood's Irregulars, jealously guarding the cattle which had been seized, were among the first to be overwhelmed by the lead elements of the iNgobamakhosi and the uVe.

What remained of Buller's command hastened after Russell and Wood. Russell's force was the first to reach Khambula, but many of Buller's command arrived hours later and into the following morning. The operation had been an absolute disaster; fifteen officers had been killed, along with seventy-nine Colonial irregulars, well over 100 of Wood's irregulars and Hamu's Zulu had also been slaughtered. As far as the Boers were concerned, the most grievous loss was Uys and what remained of the Boers left, to defend their farms that night.

Although the casualties for the Zulu are unknown, the abaQulusi undoubtedly took the brunt. The lead elements of the Zulu army had not suffered heavily, as to a large extent they were able to kill with impunity at the height of the rout.

The jubilant Zulu spent the night camped along the White Umfolozi River, between Zungwini Mountain and Nseka Hill. Although they had achieved a victory over the British and, indeed routed them, they had not yet dealt with the threat which they had been dispatched to handle by Cetshwayo. Wood's column was still

128

more or less intact, but the Zulu were supremely confident that these too would be driven from Zululand.

The three key Zulu induna, Mnyamana kaNgqengelele, Ntshingwayo kaMahole and Zibhebhu kaMaphitha, ensured that the army was fully prepared with the requisite rituals and ceremonies before moving off to the north-west, towards Khambula and Utrecht. It appears that the Zulu for manoeuvring purposes, were formed up into five columns and the advance began at around 09.00.

One of Hamu's men, who had been cut off at Hlobane, had rejoined his companions in the Zulu army. They were completely unaware that he had defected to the British. After spending much of the night with the Zulu army, he was able to slip away and report to Wood that the Zulu were on their way to destroy him. As far as Wood was concerned, although his force was heavily entrenched and within a laager, there was always the possibility that the Zulu army would simply pass him by and fall upon the completely unprotected Transvaal and the tiny garrison which protected Utrecht.

The Zulu army was spotted having a break for breakfast on the banks of a stream near Zungwini, at around 10.00. It was now apparent to Wood that the entire Zulu army was in the immediate vicinity. He still had a few precious hours to prepare.

Wood had established his laager on the crest of the Khambula Ridge and at the far eastern end he had built a second redoubt. The redoubt was surrounded by a palisade and linked to a cattle kraal, which was further reinforced with additional chained wagons. Extra barricading had been erected using sacks and boxes. All around the position, white markers had been set in the ground to mark out the ranges. The surrounding area afforded an attacking force little in the way of protection, with the possible exception of the southern approach, which featured a steep valley.

Battle focus

Khambula

29 March 1879

Wood had at his disposal six 7- pounder guns of No. 11 Battery, 7 Brigade Royal Artillery and two rocket troughs. Four of the artillery pieces were placed facing north-east between the laager and the redoubt and the remaining two pieces were placed in the redoubt. Within the main laager itself, Wood had placed eight companies of the 90th Light Infantry and seven companies of the 1st Battalion, 13th Light Infantry. A single company of the 90th and one and a half companies of the 13th were placed in the redoubt and in the cattle laager. Wood also had 500 mounted troops under the command of Buller and these were safely placed within the laager itself. They consisted of four troops of the Frontier Light Horse, two troops of Raaf's Transvaal Rangers, Baker's Horse, the Kaffarian Rifles, the Border Horse and some mounted Basutos. In addition there were a handful of Boers and Royal Engineers and around 180 of what remained of Wood's Irregulars and Hamu's warriors. In all Wood could call on 2,086 men (of whom eighty-eight were sick or wounded).

The Zulu army hove into view at around 12.00. It deployed on a sixteen kilometre front some seven kilometres to the south-east of Wood's position. The Zulu centre consisted of the iNdlondlo, the uDloko, the uThulwana, the uNdluyengwe, the iSangqu, the uDududu and the iMbube. The left horn consisted primarily of the uKhandempemvu, the uMbonambi and the uNokhenke. The right horn comprised the iNgobamakhosi and the uVe. The bulk of the Zulu army halted temporarily in order for all of the regiments to move up and get into position, but they made their advance once again at 13.00. The iNgobamakhosi and the uVe began to advance rapidly and then halted barely 1,000 metres from the laager and were

130

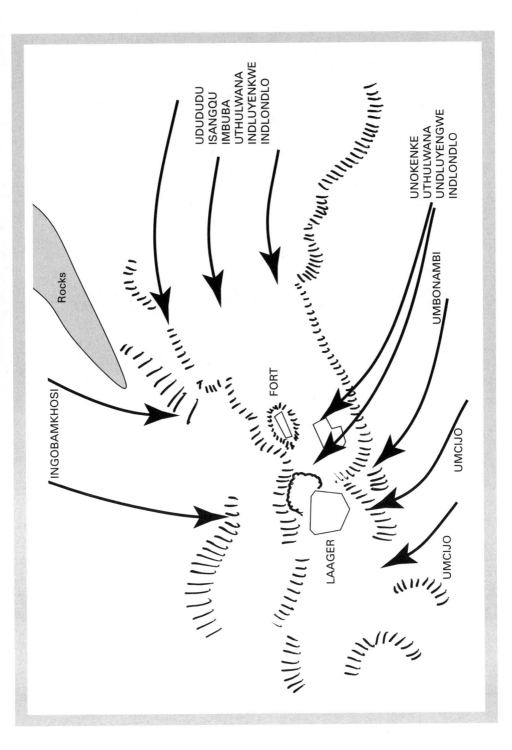

UDUDUDU
ISANGQU
IMBUBA
UTHULWANA
INDLUYENKWE
INDLONDLO

UNOKENKE
UTHULWANA
UNDLUYENGWE
INDLONDLO

UMBONAMBI

Rocks

INGOBAMKHOSI

FORT

UMCIJO

LAAGER

UMCIJO

obviously preparing themselves to attack. The left horn, meanwhile, had advanced, but it showed no signs of preparing to assault.

By now it was 13.30 and Wood seized the opportunity to provoke the iNgobamakhosi and the uVe into making a premature attack before the rest of the Zulu army was in position. He sent out Buller at the head of 100 or so mounted troops. They rode out and calmly dismounted a few hundred metres from the right horn and began to fire. Almost immediately the 6,000 warriors in the right horn broke into a run. Buller's men swiftly remounted and with the Zulu barely fifty metres behind them, galloped towards the laager. No sooner had the mounted men reached safety than the 90th, manning that side of the laager, began to open fire with crushing volleys. The attack was beaten off and the majority of the right horn fell back some 700 metres to a rocky outcrop to the east.

The Zulu commanders could see little through the palls of smoke, but realized that the right horn must be already engaged. The left horn surged forward, rolling over the dead ground until they came up the slope barely 100 metres from the laager and redoubt. The chest, meanwhile, began its approach across much more open ground.

Wood swiftly repositioned three of his artillery pieces to cover the south and as the Zulu surged over the slope they wreaked dreadful havoc among the close packed warriors. The cattle kraal was held by a company of the 13th, commanded by Captain Cox and his small force was inadequate to stop the uNokhenke from bursting into the kraal. He swiftly ordered his men to retire.

The Zulu were now among several hundred cattle, but they began to pour fire into the redoubt and the southern side of the laager. The uMbonambi began massing for an assault and Wood dispatched Major Robert Hackett, with two companies of the 90th, to break up the attack before it could develop fully. Hackett deployed his men just outside of the laager, on the slope and at 200 metres volleyed into the uMbonambi, which swiftly retired. Hackett's men were out in the open and being fired upon from Zulu who had taken up position around a rubbish heap to the west. He was also under fire from the Zulu occupying the cattle kraal. Hackett was shot through the head, but survived, despite being blinded for the rest of his life. Wood now threw out two companies of the 13th (commanded by Captain Waddy and Captain Thurlow) to cover Hackett's retreat.

No sooner had the left horn been dissuaded than the iNgobamakhosi launched another assault, supported by the uVe. A handful of the right horn managed to get close to the redoubt, but dozens were cut down by well controlled volleys and artillery fire. Once again the right horn retired back to the rocky outcrop.

For a time the focus of the battle shifted to the attacks launched by the Zulu centre. It crashed against the redoubt on several occasions but all to no avail. By around 16.40 the Zulu attacks were becoming increasingly uncoordinated, despite the fact that both the left horn and the centre were still attacking.

Wood dispatched a company of the 13th to reoccupy the cattle kraal and, at bayonet point, forced the elements of the uNonkhenke out, and down into the valley. Captain Laye's company of the 90th were then sent out to disperse the Zulu who had taken up positions in the rocks in the valley. The Zulu were now dispirited and exhausted and Wood launched Buller, at the head of the mounted troops, to ensure that the Zulu retirement was transformed into a rout. Buller's men headed first towards the Zulu right horn, mowing down scattered groups of Zulu and then driving them to the south. The British regulars and Wood's Irregulars were then sent out to assist the pursuit.

The Zulu were harried and slaughtered across sixteen kilometres for some two hours before nightfall. By then, they had passed the Zungwini Mountain; the abaQulusi headed back towards Hlobane. At approximately 19.30 the pursuit was called off and the British returned to the laager, while the Zulu army made its forlorn way to oNdini (Ulundi). Wood had lost just three officers and twenty-six other ranks killed and five officers and forty-nine men wounded. Around the laager and redoubt alone there were nearly 800 Zulu dead. Zulu losses may have been between 2, and 3,000. As devastating for the Zulu was the loss of several induna and high ranking chieftains.

By the end of March Chelmsford, after considerable difficulties, was ready to relieve Pearson, who was still besieged at Eshowe. Initially, on 25 March, he ordered reinforced patrols across the Middle Drift, the Lower Drift and Rorke's Drift. Several Zulu kraals were burned. Chelmsford began crossing into Zululand on 27 March and by the following day, with his force safely across, he began to advance. He had now collected together a considerable force, including both the 57 and the 91 Regiments, five companies of the 99th, six companies of the 3rd Battalion of the 60th Rifles, a large Naval Brigade contingent (with two Gatling guns, two 9- pounders and two rocket tubes), a large force of mounted infantry and Natal Mounted Volunteers and two reorganized and re-designated Natal Native Contingent battalions, the 4th and 5th. This time Chelmsford was not prepared to take any chances. From now on the army, moving in two columns, would prepare a laager with their 122 wagons and dig a trench and parapet around them each night.

On 1 April, Chelmsford began constructing his laager and defence works close to the Gingindlovu kraal, which Pearson had burned some weeks earlier. Reports came in that the Zulu were massing to the north and west. It was an ideal defensive position, with very little cover in the immediate vicinity. At dawn the British troops made ready for what now appeared to be the inevitable Zulu assault.

The Zulu were indeed intending to attack Chelmsford's relief column, but had hoped that they would be able to catch them on the move, rather than in a prepared position. The Zulu, under Somopho kaZikhala, had moved into the Nyezane Hills only the day before.

Battle focus

Gingindlovu

2 April 1879

Chelmsford had two brigades at his disposal, the first under Lieutenant Colonel Law. Law's command included M Battery of the 6 Brigade Royal Artillery, with two 9-pounders, two rocket tubes and a Gatling gun. He also had Naval Brigade detachments from HMS *Shah* and HMS *Tenedos*. The bulk of his regular infantry were the 91st Highlanders, backed up by five companies of the Duke of Edinburgh's 99th and two companies of the 3 Regiment (the Buffs). In total he had 1,770 white troops and 800 black troops (primarily the 4th Battalion of the Natal Native Contingent (NNC)). Chelmsford's second brigade was commanded by Lieutenant Colonel Pemberton. He had M Battery of the 7 Brigade Royal Artillery, with two rocket tubes and a Gatling gun. Pemberton also had a Naval Brigade detachment from HMS *Boadicea* along with Royal Marines from the same vessel and Royal Marines from HMS *Shah.* The bulk of his infantry were the 57 West Middlesex Regiment, six companies from the 3rd Battalion of the 60th Rifles and the 5th Battalion of the NNC. Pemberton's command amounted to 1,470 white troops and 1,200 natives. In addition, Major Barrow commanded the divisional troops consisting of mounted infantry and Natal volunteer guides (some 150 men), the Natal Native Horse (130 men) and the Native foot scouts (150 men). Along with them were 122 wagons to carry the ammunition and supplies.

Ranged against them was a mixed Zulu force, primarily commanded by Somopho kaZikhala. It is estimated that he had at least 12,000 warriors at his disposal. The core of his army was the uThulwana, the uMbonambi, the uKhandempemvu, the uVe and the iNgobamakhosi. These

135

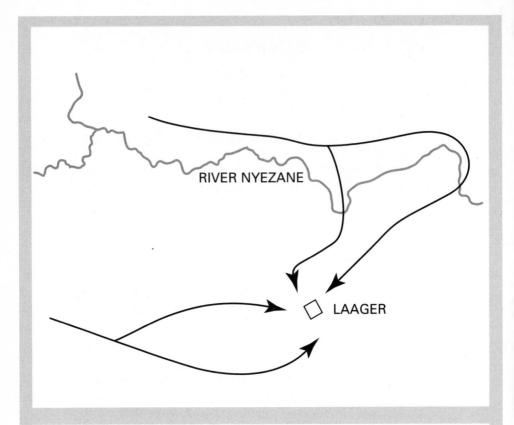

RIVER NYEZANE

LAAGER

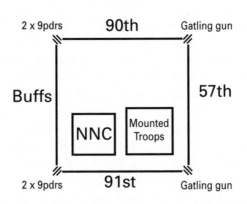

2 x 9pdrs   **90th**   Gatling gun

Buffs   **57th**

NNC   Mounted Troops

2 x 9pdrs   **91st**   Gatling gun

Gingindlovu

were supported by a number of irregular warriors from the coastal region. Somopho had subordinate commanders; Dabulamanzi kaMpande (who would lead the right horn), Sigcwelecwele kaMhlekehleke (induna of the iNgobamakhosi) and Masegwane and Mbilwane, who had both fought at Nyezane.

Chelmsford had learned the lesson of Isandlwana and had entrenched his laager the night before. At approximately 06.00 Zulu skirmishers drove in the outlying British pickets. The left horn of the Zulu army converged on the north-east corner of the laager, while the right horn assaulted the western side of the laager. British Gatling gunfire opened up at around 1,000 metres, cutting swathes through the oncoming Zulu. At around 400 metres the British regular infantry added to the weight of fire. It is believed that few Zulu got to more than thirty metres from the laager. Each time the Zulu massed to attack they were cut down and many of them sought cover in the long grass and began sniping at the laager. At this point Chelmsford ordered his mounted troops out. The dispirited Zulu began retreating towards Nyezane. Many Zulu were slaughtered as they tried to cross the river. Chelmsford then ordered the NNC to flush out any Zulu who may have been hiding in the long grass. They swiftly despatched any stragglers or wounded.

Zulu resistance had petered out after just three quarters of an hour and by 07.30 the NNC and the mounted troops had covered some three kilometres in pursuit of the Zulu. In a last, defiant gesture some of the Zulu from the right horn rallied on a hill some two kilometres from the laager, but they too were soon put to flight by artillery fire.

Chelmsford had lost just thirteen men in addition to his forty-eight wounded. Zulu casualties were in excess of 1,100, most of whom had been killed in the pursuit, although at least 4–500 were dead in the tall grass around the laager. Chelmsford could now press on to relieve Eshowe.

The following morning Chelmsford sent a Flying Column, which linked up with Pearson at Eshowe. Chelmsford had decided to evacuate the fort and organized Pearson's men to march back to Fort Pearson. Chelmsford was throwing out aggressive patrols and on 4 April they destroyed Dabulamanzi's kraal, Ezulweni, some eight miles away. Eshowe was abandoned by 6 April and only minutes afterwards the Zulu burned what was left of the fort to the ground.

The Zulu had now lost at both Khambula and Gingindlovu within days of one another. The initiative now lay with Chelmsford. He was receiving new reinforcements on a daily basis; notably he received regular British cavalry in the guise of the 1st (King's) Dragoon Guards and the 17th Lancers. Chelmsford determined that his new main column (which he dubbed the 2nd Division) would strike deep into Zululand and precipitate a final encounter with the Zulu army. Wood's column was redesignated the Flying Column and would support him, while an independent column (which he called the 1st Division) would advance along the coastal area.

Colonel H. H. Crealock, brother of J. N. Crealock (Chelmsford's Secretary) was to command the 1st Division, Edward Newdigate, the 2nd Division and Frederick Marshall was given command of the cavalry brigade (attached to the 2nd Division). To even things out, Wood became a Brigadier General. The invasion was scheduled to begin at the end of May.

There were several early incursions into Zululand, notably on 15 May when Lieutenant Colonel Black led a patrol as far as Isandlwana. Shortly afterwards the first of many visits were made to recover or bury the dead at Isandlwana.

On 20 May Major A. C. Twentyman of the 4th Foot (based at Fort Cherry) led a patrol into the Thukela Valley. Supporting his probe was a number of Border Guards and Natal Levies. Twentyman crossed the Thukela at dawn; his force amounted to around 1,000 men. They almost immediately ran into a Zulu patrol and a firefight developed, during which Twentyman fired three rockets at a hill occupied by the Zulu, dispersing them. He then proceeded to burn every kraal in the immediate vicinity and to round up cattle. Towards the end of the afternoon, as

Twentyman began moving back across into Natal, several groups of Zulu similarly crossed into Natal and destroyed a number of settlers' and natives' homesteads and kraals.

Chelmsford's 2nd Division, consisting of over 5,000 troops and 600 wagons, crossed Landman's Drift into the disputed territory on 27 May. They made for the Ncome River and into Zululand. Wood's column made similar movements in order to link up with Chelmsford deep in enemy territory.

Before the Zulu could be finally brought to battle, there was yet another major blow to Chelmsford, although perhaps more so for Imperial factions in France. On 1 June, Prince Louis Napoleon, the French exiled heir to the throne, operating in a semi-official capacity, accompanied a small group of Bettington's Natal Horse on a patrol ahead of Wood's Flying Column. The exact status of the prince still remains hotly disputed. He was a graduate of the Royal Military College at Woolwich and at least officially, a lieutenant. Accompanying Louis and six other men was Lieutenant Jahleel Brenton Carey (98 Regiment). It was as unclear as it is now who assumed command. Be that as it may, the patrol, ostensibly searching for signs of Chelmsford's column and of Zulu movement, halted to make coffee close to the Itshotshosi River in what appeared to be an abandoned Zulu kraal. There were clear signs that the kraal had been hastily abandoned, yet the men took little precaution and settled down for their break. Suddenly, a scouting party (with men from the iNgobamakhosi, uMbonambi and the uNokhenke regiments) ran into them. In the ensuing chaos Louis was among those killed. Carey's conduct was to blight him for the rest of his short life.

By 5 June Chelmsford and Wood had reached the Nondweni River. The Zulu were concentrating in the immediate area. Later in the day the 17th Lancers would have their first taste of action, when they ran into Zulu patrols near the uPoko River. On 6 June Chelmsford began constructing Fort Newdigate.

Meanwhile, Cetshwayo had hoped to secure a negotiated settlement. He had deferred calling up the army once more until June, but by the end of that month some 20,000 men had answered his call and were concentrated around oNdini (Ulundi). There still seemed to be considerable fight left in the Zulu, despite the fact that Magwendu kaMpande had surrendered to the British in late April and there were rumours that Dabulamanzi and Mavumengwane kaNdlela were about to surrender.

A peace mission from Cetshwayo had arrived at Chelmsford's Nondweni stronghold on 4 June. Chelmsford met with them on 5 June, telling them bluntly that the king must surrender all of his cattle and all muskets in the kingdom and return the two artillery pieces taken from Isandlwana. He also decreed that a token Zulu regiment should march to Nondweni and lay down their arms before him. Cetshwayo was duly informed, but again there was no possibility that he could comply.

Back in London moves were afoot to replace Chelmsford, as the government and top military circles refused to be associated with a man who had brought about the disaster at Isandlwana. Chelmsford was to be replaced by General Sir Garnet Wolseley, a man with a considerable reputation. He arrived in Cape Town on 23 June and almost immediately boarded a vessel for Durban. He was determined to be in command of the army as it approached oNdini. It was not to be; by 26 June the British were raiding deep into emaKhosini Valley, the very heartland of the Zulu nation.

One of the kraals destroyed by the 17th Lancers, and subsequently others burned down by the column itself, at esiKlebheni, contained the sacred Zulu grass rope coil wrapped in python skin. It was the most sacred object of the Zulu and its destruction psychologically spelled disaster for the kingdom.

By the following day Chelmsford's column had reached the Mthonjaneni Ridge. The invaders could now see the White Unfolozi Valley and the Mhlabathini Plain, upon which oNdini lay. Once again a Zulu peace envoy arrived, with elephant tusks and 150 cattle which he said had been taken at Isandlwana. The Zulu implored Chelmsford to believe that Cetshwayo wanted peace, but he turned him down and simply repeated his previous demands. He did, however, undertake not to cross the Umfolozi. In actual fact Chelmsford was not ready to cross the Umfolozi, as his men were busy preparing a final staging post at Mthonjaneni Ridge.

It was clearly Cetshwayo's earnest desire to at least secure a temporary halt to the British advance and as Chelmsford's men began entering the Umfolozi Valley on 30 June, another Zulu peace mission arrived. They had brought with them Prince Louis Napoleon's sword. This time Chelmsford offered to rescind the demand that a Zulu regiment surrender. Instead he demanded the return of the Martini-Henrys which had been taken at Isandlwana. He further promised that he would not cross the Umfolozi River until 3 July.

Meanwhile, Wolseley had reached Durban on 28 June. He immediately sent instructions to Chelmsford to cease offensive actions and to await him in the field. Wolseley was determined to be in command when the final battle against the Zulu was fought. He had a choice; either to join the 1st Division or the 2nd Division. He chose the 1st but was unable to land at Port Durnford and returned to Durban with the intention of linking up with Crealock, but by then Chelmsford had brought the Zulu army to battle and defeated it at oNdini.

On 1 July it appeared that the Zulu were manoeuvring to attack, but as it transpired Cetshwayo had ordered the army simply to resist Chelmsford's attempts to cross the Umfolozi, but not to launch a full scale attack. As the British troops crossed the drift they came under fire from Zulu snipers positioned there by Zibhebhu kaMaphitha. On the following day Cetshwayo sent a large herd of his own white royal cattle as a gesture of peace. But the Khandempemvu regiment refused to allow the cattle through their lines.

3 July dawned and at midday Chelmsford dispatched Buller, at the head of a mounted force, to scout an ideal position for the column to set up and force a battle. The mounted men forced the Zulu snipers out of their positions and Buller's men pursued them towards the Mbilane stream. Zibhebhu had set a trap for Buller and as they reached the stream Buller found himself virtually surrounded by up to 10,000 Zulu. They had prepared the ground well and had plaited the long grass to trip the horses. The first Zulu volley ripped into Buller's mounted troops and it was only by luck that he had left a troop behind him that allowed them to cover his retreat. The Zulu pursued him back towards the drift. Despite the near disaster, an ideal site to advance had been identified; it was a low ridge to the west of the oNdini kraal, past the ruins of kwaBulawayo and kwaNodwengu.

141

Chelmsford resolved to advance across the Umfolozi the following morning. He dispatched his mounted troops across the Lower Drift at 06.00. They seized the ridges above the Upper Drift and the main force began crossing at 06.45. A small force was left to guard the forward camp. Chelmsford had with him over 4,000 white troops, nearly 1,000 natives, twelve artillery pieces, two Gatling guns and a rocket battery. The army crossed the drift and entered the Mahlabathini Plain with two days' rations and only ammunition as supplies. As soon as they had dropped down onto the plain, Chelmsford formed a large, hollow rectangle. It was now around 07.30 and they proceeded slowly across the plain towards the chosen battle site.

Battle focus

oNdini (Ulundi)

4 July 1879

Chelmsford had both the 2nd Division, under Newdigate, and the Flying Column, under Wood. Newdigate's division consisted of the King's Dragoon Guards, the 17th Lancers (Duke of Cambridge's Own), N Battery of the 6 Brigade Royal Artillery with six 9- pounders, N Battery of the 5 Brigade Royal Artillery with two 7- pounders, the 2nd Battalion of the 21st Royal Scots Fusiliers, the 58 Regiment (Rutlandshire), the 94 Regiment, the 2nd Battalion Natal Native Contingent (NNC) and Shepstone's and Bettington's Horse.

Wood's column consisted of No. 11 Battery, 7 Brigade of the Royal Artillery with four 7- pounders, No. 10 Battery, 7 Brigade with two Gatling guns, a small detachment of Royal Engineers, 1st Battalion 13th Light Infantry, the 80 Regiment (Staffordshire Volunteers), 90th Light Infantry, the Natal Native Pioneers, Wood's irregulars, Mounted Infantry, the Transvaal Rangers, the Frontier and Natal Light Horse and the Natal Native Horse. By 08.00 the square was in position. The Zulu had mustered between 15, and 20,000 men, with

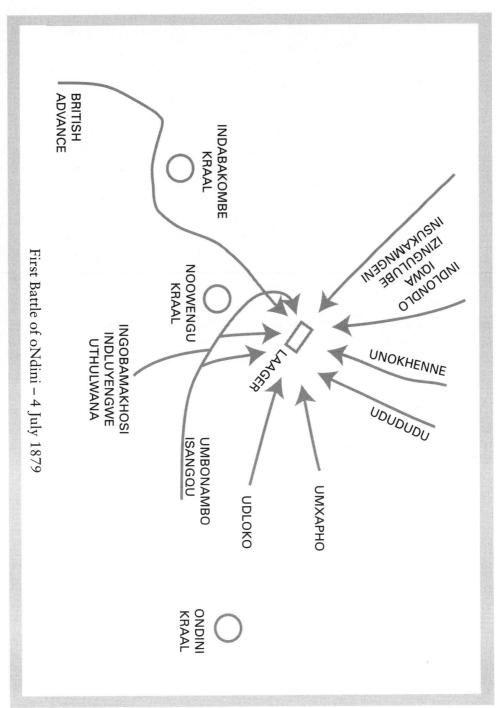

INDABAKOMBE
KRAAL

BRITISH
ADVANCE

NOOWENGU
KRAAL

INGOBAMAKHOSI
INDLUYENGWE
UTHULWANA

INSUKAMNGENI
IZINGULUBE
IOWA
INDLONDLO

UNOKHENNE

LAAGER

UDUDUDU

UMBONAMBO
ISANGQU

UDLOKO

UMXAPHO

ONDINI
KRAAL

First Battle of oNdini – 4 July 1879

a further 5,000 in reserve. Cetshwayo was not present; he had left oNdini the day before and had left the conduct of the battle in the hands of his brother, Ziwedu kaMpande and the experienced indunas, Mnyamana, Dabulamanzi and Ntshingwayo. The Zulu army formed up in the traditional manner. The centre consisted of the iNdlondo, the iQwa, the izinGulube, the iNsukamngeni, the uNokhenke and the uDududu. The Zulu left horn consisted of the umXapho, the uDloko, the uMbonambi, the iSangqu, the uThulwana, the iNdluyengwe, the iNgobamakhosi and the uVe. The right horn comprised the umCijo.

Chelmsford was determined to provoke a Zulu attack and sent out Buller to goad the enemy regiments. A few shots were traded but the cavalry retreated back into the square just as the artillery began to open fire. It was around 08.45. The entire Zulu army, which was lacking cover, surged around the square. At around 400 metres the British infantry began ripping into the Zulu with devastating volleys. The Gatling guns then opened up. A handful of Zulu managed to get within thirty metres of the square but most of them sought cover in order to avoid the punishing fire. With no defensive earthworks or wagons, the British were comparatively exposed, but very few casualties were inflicted. The Zulu were unable to make any headway and were taking heavy casualties.

The indunas quickly realized that the weak spots were the corners and the iNgobamakhosi and the uVe made for what remained of the uNodwengu kraal, where they began to fire on the corner of the square. The bulk of the rest of the Zulu army had retreated out of rifle range. The iNgobamakhosi and the uVe launched an attack on the right corner of the square. They were able to get in very close before the shrapnel from the artillery managed to break up the attack. This time the Zulu had got to within ten metres.

There was one final advance from the Zulu from the direction of oNdini, but artillery fire broke up this attack before it developed fully.

Shortly after 09.00 the bulk of the Zulu army was pinned down and seemed reluctant to close. Just twenty minutes later the British could see many Zulu retiring. At 09.35 Chelmsford ordered the 17th Lancers, to be followed by Buller's mounted men, out of the square. The cavalry gave no quarter and any little knots of resistance were broken up by the charging horsemen or artillery fire.

It had been a short and ruinous engagement. Upwards of 1,500 Zulu had been killed, a large number of whom had been dispatched in the pursuit. Three British officers and ten other ranks had been killed and nineteen officers had been wounded, as had sixty-nine other ranks. It was the crushing victory which Chelmsford had sought partially to redeem himself for the disaster at Isandlwana.

Wood, meanwhile, on the same day as oNdini, had accepted the surrender of Somopho kaZikhala, who had commanded the warriors at the battle of Gingindlovu, as well as Somkhele kaMalanda, arguably the most powerful tribal chieftain in the coastal area.

Chelmsford received notice that Wolseley was to take over from him on 5 July. He had already ordered his troops to retire. Wolseley reached the 1st Division on 7 July and pushed the column on to St Paul's. Having already resigned his command, Chelmsford met him at St Paul's on 16 July. By the 21st Chelmsford was in Pietermartizburg and by the 27th he had set sail for England from Durban.

Wolseley was left with the difficult task of pacifying the rest of the kingdom and, above all, capturing Cetshwayo. On 18 July he ordered two small columns to enter the centre of Zululand and send out patrols to find the king. Already detachments of the British army were leaving the region, bound for other duties around the world. The first of Wolseley's columns, under the command of Lieutenant Colonel Clarke, established a base near oNdini and were charged with hunting down Cetshwayo. A second column was sent into northern Zululand to ensure the submission of Manyanyoba and the abaQulusi. In a meeting with several Zulu chiefs on 19 July, Wolseley informed them that the Zulu regimental system was to be disbanded and that Cetshwayo was to lose his crown.

Cetshwayo was on his way north and it seems that he intended to re-establish a royal kraal near the Swazi border. He tried with no avail to muster several of his regiments; they refused to respond to his call.

Clarke had dispatched a sizeable mounted patrol to comb northern Zululand, but they found no trace of Cetshwayo. The greater part of the expedition, under Major Barrow, returned to oNdini, but a small group was left under the command of Major Lord Gifford. For several days he hunted the king to the north of the Black Umfolozi River. On 26 August Clarke received news that Cetshwayo was in the region of the Ngome forest and immediately dispatched Major Marter with mounted troops to check out the rumour. Meanwhile Gifford had also received news that this was indeed the whereabouts of Cetshwayo. Early in the morning of 28 August Marter's group found a small kraal which he believed was housing Cetshwayo. He sent some Native Auxiliaries down a steep slope, while the rest of his party entered the valley by another route. With the kraal surrounded, Marter's men approached; they had found the Zulu monarch.

Cetshwayo was finally brought into the camp at oNdini on 31 August 1879. He was destined, at least for now, to suffer the indignity of exile.

Chapter Nine

Restoration

From the outset, Wolseley laboured under the misapprehension that Zululand was nothing more than a confederation of different tribes, brutally moulded together by the Zulu monarch. Wolseley proposed, on 1 September 1879, at oNdini, where he had summoned some 200 chieftains, that the kingdom would be divided into thirteen separate kingdoms. Wolseley laid down a series of conditions which had fundamental implications. There was to be no military establishment, men could marry as they chose, the chieftains' people could offer themselves for work in Transvaal or Natal, or indeed move there if they wished. There was to be no importation of muskets or weapons and there was to be no summary executions; lives could not be taken without trial. Any individual wanted by the British was to be surrendered and British subjects could not be tried by native courts. The chieftains could not sell or exchange their land and no major decision, including war or succession, could be prosecuted without the permission of the British resident. Wolseley then went on to choose his thirteen chieftains.

Cetshwayo, meanwhile, had been hastened from oNdini, escorted by two companies of British infantry and two troops of Volunteer Horse. By 4 September he had been conveyed to Port Durnford, where he was taken aboard *The Natal*. He now realized, to his horror, that he would not be exiled in Natal but in a more distant land. He was first conveyed to Cape Town, where, wearing a European suit and a black hat, he was passed into the care of Colonel Fairfax Hassard. Cetshwayo was to stay in an apartment at the Old Dutch Castle, where he would remain for nearly three years.

John Dunn had been one individual who had profited well from Wolseley's partitioning of Zululand. He was given a vast area, including his former lands near the coast, but also large stretches along the Thukela. In effect, this created a buffer zone between Natal and the rest of Zululand. Within his domain were the territories of Dabulamanzi. Hamu kaNzibe had also profited, given the fact that he had gone over to Wood early in the war. He was given control of most of the north-west of the country. Hamu had the difficulty of having the abaQulusi within his territory.

Another man, who had been entirely faithful to Cetshwayo during the war, was also given most of northern Zululand. This man, Zibhebhu kaMaphitha, a direct descendent of Senzanga-khona's brother, was further given control of Cetshwayo's heir, Dinuzulu, in addition to Cetshwayo's brother, Ndabuko and his half-brother, Ziwedu.

The first British resident, Wheelwright, established himself at Eshowe. He swiftly resigned, on account of the fact that he felt powerless, and he was replaced in March 1880 by Melmoth Osborn, who had worked for Shepstone in the Transvaal.

Meanwhile, Zulu royalists were beginning to flex their muscles. There were accusations that Zibhebhu was mistreating Dinuzulu and Ndabuko. There were constant skirmishes and squabbles in Zibhebhu's kingdom and Hamu's, between their supporters and the uSuthu royalist supporters. In February 1880 representatives of the king visited Natal with a bound copy of the speeches which Shepstone had made at Cetshwayo's coronation. They wanted clarification as to which of the promises Cetshwayo had broken. The Zulu representatives then made their way to Pietermaritzburg, in order to see John Shepstone, who simply passed them on to Osborn, who was now in post. Osborn refused to listen, particularly to the complaints regarding Zibhebhu's treatment of the Zulu royals. It seems that Cetshwayo was completely aware of the political moves being made on his behalf. He also had a number of white supporters in southern Africa and they were trying to secure permission for Cetshwayo to travel to London to plead his cause.

1881 saw further confusion in Zululand, with Ndabuko demanding that Hamu return 2,000 cattle which belonged to him. A man named Sitimela appeared in Godide kaNdlela's kingdom and announced that he was none other than Dingiswayo's grandson. On this pretext he seized hundreds of head of cattle and then brought together a small army and forced Ndlela out, making him flee into John Dunn's territory. By now, of the thirteen kingdoms, only Dunn, Hamu, Zibhebhu and Fanawendhlela were still in opposition to Cetshwayo's return.

In August 1881 Evelyn Wood called a meeting of the Zulu chieftains and the royal supporters in order to attempt to diffuse the situation. He told the Zibhebhu to return a third of the cattle which he had taken from Ndabuko and Ziwedu, on the proviso that Ndabuko and Ziwedu, along with Dinuzulu, moved into John Dunn's territory. Hamu was ordered to return around half of the cattle he had taken from Mnyamana. The meeting broke up and Zibhebhu hurried home to seize all of the uSuthu cattle before they could be taken to Dunn, but he was forced away by a neighbouring chieftain. Dunn, meanwhile, took as many of the cattle belonging to the royal family as he could, the moment they entered his territory. Hamu now ran into difficulties with Mnyamana and the abaQulusi. He decided on a pre-emptive strike and burned their kraals and drove them out of his territory. Meanwhile, with the connivance of Osborn, Dunn attacked Sitimela (who was believed in fact to be simply a usurper and a Natal native). Sitimela's followers were scattered and Ndlela was restored to power.

Cetshwayo had been kept fully apprised of the developments and had recently been moved to a farm called Oude Moulen, on the outskirts of Cape Town. He rekindled his friendship with Langalibalele, who was the exiled amaHlubi chieftain. Cetshwayo was still agitating to meet Queen Victoria, but he would have some time to wait.

Finally Cetshwayo was given leave to travel to London to press his claims and he arrived in England on 12 July 1882. He had retained his regal appearance, wore European clothing and rented a house in Kensington. He was finally given leave to meet the

Queen at Osborne House and discuss matters with the Colonial Office on 7 August. Whether the Colonial Office actually wanted a reunified royal Zululand is unclear, but it was agreed that Cetshwayo would be given a part of Zululand, without control over Dunn, Zibhebhu, Hamu or the other anti-monarchist, Fanawendhlela. By 24 September Cetshwayo was back at Oude Moulen. He would still have to wait until the Governor of Natal and Special Commissioner for Zululand, Sir Henry Bulwer, had sorted out all of the details.

Amongst the complications was the re-jigging of the territory. Dunn would lose the bulk of his lands, Ndabuko and Ziwedu would be given back their kraals, which would be incorporated into Cetshwayo's area. This meant that Zibhebhu would also lose land, but he was compensated by being given more territory in the north. This territory was nominally owned by Mgojana and contained many of the most ardent uSuthu clans. Bulwer decided to incorporate Hamu's territory into Cetshwayo's land; this was to be one of the most difficult problems to overcome, particularly given the fact that Mnyama and abaQuluzi were distinctly pro-royalist.

Cetshwayo finally landed at Port Durnford on 10 January 1883, having been brought there by HMS *Briton*. Theophilus Shepstone was waiting there for him. Cetshwayo's restoration officially took place on 29 January 1883. In attendance at the ceremony on the Mthonjaneni Heights, overlooking emaKhosini Valley, were the Mnyamana, Buthelezi, Ndabuko and Dabulamanzi, amongst others; Zibhebhu and Hamu refused to attend, despite the former arriving and paying his respects to Shepstone before absenting himself.

Cetshwayo was faced with a ravaged land. Nonetheless he rebuilt oNdini, little more than a mile to the east of his former royal kraal. No sooner had Cetshwayo been reinstalled than the abaQuluzi began raiding Hamu's kraals. Zibhebhu also suffered raids from uSuthu clans in his region.

Towards the end of March 1883 Mnyamana and Ndabuko had assembled around 5,000 men to launch an assault on Bangonomo Zibhebhu's major kraal. The uSuthu marched into the Mseb Valley on 30 March; they considerably outnumbered Zibhebhu, who had, perhaps, no more than 2,000 men. Zibhebhu, however, was a wily and dangerous opponent. He intended to ambush the larger force and as the uSuthu approached, Zibhebhu pretended to retreat, luring them into difficult terrain cut by dongas and ridges. Just as the uSuthu thought they had won an almost bloodless victory, Zibhebhu ambushed them and overran their lead elements. The royalists were caught completely unawares and their resistance collapsed. Zibhebhu ruthlessly sought out the fleeing enemy and it is said that 4,000 uSuthu were dead before darkness drew in.

The initiative now lay with Zibhebhu and Hamu, who harried the royalists wherever they were. Mnyamana tried without success to depose Hamu. Cetshwayo's position was difficult; he could not be seen to be openly supporting the uSuthu, but by July the entire country was blighted with civil war and Osborn was powerless to do anything about it. He blamed Cetshwayo, but the British refused to be drawn into the conflict militarily.

Much to Osborn's alarm, Cetshwayo had been mustering his supporters at oNdini. He dispatched Ndabuko and Mnyamana to the north to link up with the uSuthu supporters in the region. Meanwhile Cetshwayo's army at oNdini was growing. In terms of the military system of Zululand, although Cetshwayo had tried to reform many of his old regiments, a large number from each regiment were, in fact, fighting for Zibhebhu and Hamu. Nonetheless, the king could rely on the bulk of the iNgobamakhosi, the uKhandempemvu, the uThulwana, the uDloko, the uNokhenke, the uMxapho, the iSangqu, the iMbube and the uDududu. He had also created a new regiment, the uFalaza.

It should be remembered that without the regiments' military kraals, the warriors bore little resemblance to the forces which had been arrayed against Chelmsford in 1879. The royalists, however, identified themselves by wearing a piece of white cowhide over the forehead, with the tail of a cow attached (tshokobezi).

Most of the notable Zulu induna were also present. Ntshingwayo kaMahole commanded the uDloko, Godide kaNdlela the uMxapho, Hayiyana kaMaphitha (Zibhebhu's brother) the uThulwana, the uKhandempemvu was led by Vumandaba kaNtati and, in addition, Dabulamanzi, Ziwedu and

151

Sitheku were present. Cetshwayo's force did not expect Zibhebhu to launch an assault on oNdini but expected him to strike against the uSuthu in the north (led by Ndabuko and Mnyamana).

Zibhebhu could call upon some 3,000 warriors and had mustered his force at his ekuVukeni kraal on the Nongoma Ridge on 20 July. Despite Cetshwayo's belief that he would not be the target of an attack, Zibhebhu was marching straight for oNdini.

Zibhebhu's Mandlakazi were spotted some five miles from oNdini by the royalists. The royalists were by no means prepared, but they were quickly roused and took precious time to begin to organize themselves into their regiments. It was proposed that the king should flee, but Cetshwayo refused. By the time the majority of the royalists were formed up, Zibhebhu was barely a mile away.

Battle focus

The second battle of oNdini (Ulundi)

21 July 1883

The uSuthu had been caught sufficiently unawares that the kwaNodwengu regiments (the iSangqu, the iMbube and the uDududu) were still some miles to the west. Therefore the uThulwana, the uDloko, the uMxapho and the uNokhenke took up the centre, while the iNgobamakhosi and the uKhandempemvu formed the right horn and the uFalaza the left horn.

The Mandlakazi hit the uSuthu right horn and their resistance swiftly collapsed; they routed towards the White Umfolozi Valley. Zibhebhu's centre, made up of some of his Mandlakazi and Hamu's Ngenetsheni, poured towards the royalist's centre. It, too, broke before contact was even made; some made a stand and among the casualties was Godide kaNdlela. The uFalaza immediately broke and the whole uSuthu force was streaming back in confusion towards oNdini. Zibhebhu's men poured into the kraal and in the confused fighting what remained of the uThulwani were slaughtered, including Vumandaba. Zibhebhu's men

152

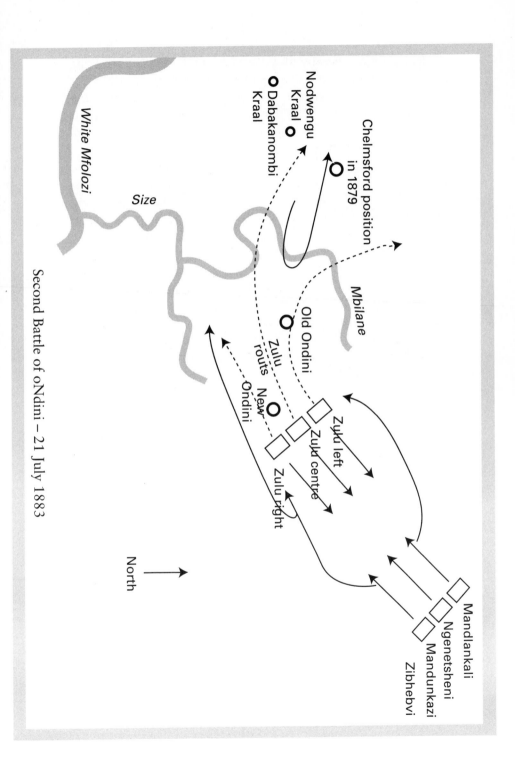

White Mfolozi

Size

Nodwengu
Kraal

Dabakanombi
Kraal

Chelmsford position
in 1879

Mbilane

Old Ondini

Zulu
routs

New
Ondini

Zulu left

Zulu centre

Zulu right

Mandlankali

Ngenetsheni

Mandunkazi

Zibhebvi

North

Second Battle of oNdini – 21 July 1883

also slaughtered any man they saw and soon the royalists were fleeing across the Mahlabathini Plain. Unluckily for them, the Mandlakazi left horn had cut them off from the river. Suddenly the Nodwengu regiments arrived, but their resolve was immediately broken at the sight of the rest of their army fleeing.

Cetshwayo had escaped and was hiding near the Ntukwini stream. He was spotted by the Mandlakazi and was hit twice in the leg by thrown spears. In danger of being killed, Cetshwayo now shouted to his assailants, one of whom he recognized. Immediately the Mandlakazi dropped their weapons and saluted the king; they then helped to take the spears out of his thigh, apologizing profusely for having attacked him. They even helped him clean his wound and then showed him the safest route from the battlefield.

Some of the other royalist notables had also escaped, including importantly Dinuzulu and Dabulamanzi. Ntshingwayo, the man who had wrought the victory for the Zulu at Isandlwana was dead, to add to the losses of Godide, Vumandaba, Hayiyana and Nyoniyentaba (Cetshwayo's younger son).

Exact losses at the second battle of oNdini are difficult to unravel. To put the royalist losses into perspective, upwards of sixty key royalist individuals had been killed and certainly the slaughter among the regiments or parts of regiments who had tried to make a stand were enormous. Zibhebhu had suffered extremely low casualties. He looted oNdini and set if afire, rounded up cattle and captives (including Sitheku) and headed back towards his own territory.

Cetshwayo, whose wounds were not that serious, hid for a short while in the White Umfolozi Valley. He then headed to Eshowe to seek the protection of Osborn. By October, with the uSuthu clans virtually overrun across the whole of the country by Zibhebhu and Hamu, Cetshwayo surrendered to the British. For a short while Cetshwayo remained in the immediate vicinity of Eshowe. The Colonial Office was desperately trying to reach some kind of solution within the Zulu kingdom. Then, on 8 February 1884, Cetshwayo suddenly died.

Osborn was immediately called and a doctor indeed proclaimed Cetshwayo dead; his relatives would not allow an autopsy and the official cause of death was a heart attack. It is strongly believed, however, that Cetshwayo had been poisoned. He was buried near Sigananda kaSokufa's kraal close to the Nkandla forest, to the north of the Thukela Valley.

At the time of Cetshwayo's death his Great Wife was pregnant and after his death she gave birth to a son, Manzolwandhle. Theoretically, at least, he had a greater claim to the throne than Dinuzulu, who was now sixteen years old. The two principle royalist figures, Ndabuko and Mnyamana, quickly realized that they must throw their support behind Dinuzulu. As a result, the newly born son was moved to Natal and played no further role in his deceased father's kingdom. The British, meanwhile, were still determined not to become embroiled in what had become a purging of the uSuthu throughout Zululand. The most they would commit themselves to was the placing of garrisons to protect the Natal border. The uSuthu could turn only to the other remaining force in the region, the Boer.

Dinuzulu slipped into the Transvaal in April 1884. This seemed to confirm that the uSuthu and the Boers had come to some arrangement. Dabulamanzi, shortly after hearing that the uSuthu had come to terms with the Boers, launched an attack on the Reserve Commissioner's camp, but was beaten off by the Reserve Territory Carbineers. Officially, at least, the Transvaal government was keen to distance themselves from any formal arrangement with Dinuzulu. Nonetheless at least 200 Boers offered their services to the young heir. As the days passed, more Boers and adventurers flocked to Dinuzulu's cause on the assumption that their support would lead to them being granted land should Dinuzulu's claim to the throne come to fruition.

On 21 May 1884, near the battlefield of Hlobane, the Boers proclaimed Dinuzulu King of the Zulu and pledged that they would support and protect him. There were at least 9,000 loyal Zulu supporters present, in addition to some 350 Boers and other adventurers. There was absolutely no way that Zibhebhu would recognize Dinuzulu as king and foolishly the new monarch promised farms to any Boer who would help him recover his father's kingdom. Meanwhile, word was sent out to the scattered uSuthu to muster to deal with Zibhebhu and his Mandlakazi.

Zibhebhu could still rely on Hamu, but his requests for assistance to Dunn were rebuffed, as were his appeals to the British. It now seemed that the momentum had definitely passed to Dinuzulu and only a handful of Zibhebhu's white allies stayed with him. One such man, Johan Colenbrander, placed an advertisement in Natal in a newspaper, which read:

> All able-bodied men of good character who can ride and shoot well are required at once. Applicants must be prepared to provide their own horse, carbine, etc. such as they may require for field service. Satisfactory remuneration offered.

The advertisement attracted probably around ten men and even then the Natal government stepped in and forced these men to return home.

By the beginning of June the uSuthu had mustered some 7,000 warriors. They were supported by Lucas Meyer, at the head of 120 Boer. They marched to Mnyamana's kraal, close to Zibhebhu's territory. They made straight for Zibhebhu's main kraal at Bangonomo, arriving there on 3 June, only to find it deserted. Zibhebhu was retreating to the north-east and the Boer and uSuthu gave chase. By 5 June they had reached the Mkhuze River. It was an ideal spot for an ambush; Zibhebhu's speciality.

Battle focus

eTshaneni

5 June 1884

Zibhebhu had deployed his 3,000 warriors and a small group of white allies on the hills overlooking the Mkhuze River to the south. He had taken with him virtually his entire civilian population and a vast herd of cattle, believed to have

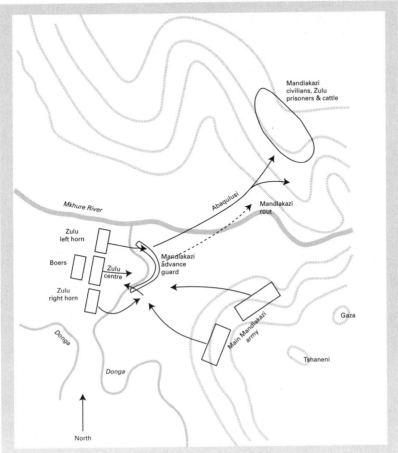

eTshaneni 5 June 1884

numbered 60,000. The non-combatants and cattle were placed in the hills to the north of the river. Zibhebhu deployed the bulk of his troops along the rocky ridges known as eTshaneni and Gaza. He had placed a blocking force alongside a donga, close to the river; his intention was that the pursuing uSuthu and Boers would be engaged by this forward force, believing it to be the whole of his army. At the appropriate time he would unleash the bulk of his force down the ridge and catch the enemy unawares.

As things transpired, Dinuzulu's force was perfectly well aware that he had entered territory ideal for an ambush and had taken the necessary precautions by deploying into battle formation. Mamese commanded the left horn, which was principally made up of uSuthu and abaQulusi and a dozen or more Boers. They were closest to the south bank of the river. The right horn was scouting ahead further to the south. The centre contained the bulk of the uSuthu warriors, supported by Meyer's Boers.

Both the left and right horn reached the donga at about the same time and were immediately attacked by the Mandlakazi forward units. Zibhebhu's plan had been for the advanced guard to break off and appear to rout towards his main positions, where he had hoped to catch the uSuthu disorganized and in pursuit. Before the advance guard could break off, however, a shot was fired from Zibhebhu's main position, which immediately alerted the uSuthu to the danger. Zibhebhu's main body, believing this to be the signal to attack, began surging down the ridge towards Dinuzulu's force.

The Mandlakazi drove back the uSuthu right horn and began pressurizing its centre. As the centre appeared to begin to crack, Meyer ordered his men to volley into the milling mass, killing friend and foe alike. Nonetheless the uSuthu were heartened by the support and the Mandlakazi were checked.

The Boers continued to fire and it was the Mandlakazi left horn which began to fall back. The Boers now concentrated their fire, supported by the reinvigorated uSuthu, on the Mandlakazi centre. Many of the Mandlakazi were trapped in the donga, whilst others began fleeing towards the river.

The drift was deep across the Mkhuze and it was difficult to cross. If the Mandlakazi had any remaining resolve to fight, this was quickly quenched by the abaQulusi, who swiftly crossed the river and began intercepting the fugitives. The abaQulusi's charge took them up the ridge, where they discovered the Mandlakazi civilians and the

158

cattle. Among the non-combatants were many uSuthu women who had been taken by the Mandlakazi in raids in the past. The abaQulusi began indiscriminately slaughtering all of the Mandlakazi civilians, but Zibhebhu had escaped.

Again it is difficult to judge the number of casualties on either side, but certainly the numbers were significant on both sides. As for the Boers, they had not lost a single man. What remained of the Mandlakazi was streaming to the north, but the uSuthu were more concerned with rounding up the cattle.

The Boers, after the victory, were not slow in coming forward with their requests for farms which Dinuzulu had foolishly offered. The Boers collectively demanded three million acres of land; in other words, the majority of the north of Zululand. Some 800 Boers lay claim to farms. Dinuzulu officially signed the transfer of the land to the Boers on 16 August 1884, much to the horror of the Zulu people.

Zibhebhu, meanwhile, had headed for Eshowe to seek the protection of the British Commissioner and in September around a third of the Mandlakazi, amounting to some 5, or 6,000 individuals, made the long trek across Zululand and into the Reserve Territory.

Chapter Ten

Dinuzulu

The British recognized the Boer New Republic on 22 October 1886. The new Boer state's capital was at Vryheid (freedom), between Hlobane and Khambula. Not once were the Zulu consulted and Dinuzulu complained bitterly, but his complaints fell on deaf ears.

In February 1887 Dinuzulu was informed that what remained of Zululand would become a British protectorate on 9 May. This would incorporate what little land Dinuzulu had left, as well as the Reserve Territory. The British continued to refuse to recognize Dinuzulu as the monarch of the Zulu and indeed they allowed Zibhebhu to reclaim his old territory in northern Zululand. This, they felt, would at least act as a foil against the royalists. By that time, however, the majority of his kraals had been occupied by the uSuthu and he now took immediate steps to evict them.

Dinuzulu had to support his uSuthu and the king's supporters were becoming increasingly belligerent and unwilling to vacate Zibhebhu's kraals. Zibhebhu appealed to the local British magistrate to have them evicted and in March 1888 a British official arrived with eight black troopers, the Nongqai (police), to evict a uSuthu chieftain. He was faced with over 1,000 armed Zulu. The official and the trooper withdrew, reported to Osborn, who promptly issued warrants for the arrests of Ndabuko and Dinuzulu. The warrants were to be served on 1 June and Osborn left Eshowe at the head of sixty-four Nongqai, supported by 140 British regulars from Natal and 400 of Mnyamana's Zulu. They encountered a uSuthu force of 1,800 and there was a vicious skirmish, during which two of the British force were killed. Dinuzulu had been forced into a corner and, presumably under his instructions, two white traders were killed (a father and son who had acted as guides for the British column). Dinuzulu then attacked Zibhebhu's Mandlakazi. Worse was to come.

A uSuthu army attacked the Nongqai garrison at Nongoma. Zibhebhu attempted to assist the garrison, but he was defeated at a battle at Ndunu Hill and the Mandlakazi was scattered. In July Osborn had mustered 2,200 men and on 2 July he defeated Shingana (Dinuzulu's uncle) at the cost of just over sixty casualties. Dinuzulu's brief rebellion had been crushed and he, his uncle and Ndabuko fled to Vryheid. The Boers would not accept their surrender, or protect them and they had no other choice but to give themselves up in Natal. During October there was a long and complicated trial at Eshowe and the result was inevitable. Ndabuko was sentenced to fifteen years, Shingana to twelve and Dinuzulu to ten years. At the beginning of 1889 the three men were deported to St Helena. Zibhebhu was also charged, but acquitted and placed in exile, along with his tribe, in the reserve.

For the next ten years or so there was relative peace. The country was being gradually developed; settlers were establishing themselves across the country, traders were widespread and roads were being built to connect the more major kraals and settlements. John Dunn died in August 1895, leaving his territory to be something of a problem. In November 1897 Tongaland was annexed and made part of Zululand and on 30 December 1897 the new combined territory became part of Natal.

Dinuzulu finally returned home in January 1898. He was given a small reserve of his own and Zibhebhu was allowed to return to his northern homeland, where he would die in relative peace in 1905. The Zulu who were living in the New Republic had been forcibly removed from their lands. They had no rights and worked as virtual slaves for the Boers. There was extreme tension between the Zulu and the Boers in the New Republic.

When the first Anglo Boer War broke out in 1899, it was unclear which way the Zulu would turn. The British certainly wanted them to remain neutral and shortly after the outbreak of the war the Boers sent a delegation to Dinuzulu's new royal kraal, oSuthu, requesting that they remain out of the war. The war certainly precipitated a mass exodus of Zulu from the New Republic.

The British had slightly changed their attitude towards Dinuzulu and the Zulu. They could see that he was still a powerful symbol and in June 1900, A. J. Shepstone, the son of Theophilius Shepstone, in collaboration with the Assistant British Military Intelligence Officer, J. Roberts, began carefully approaching the Zulu. The British had occupied Vryheid in June 1900 and the two men began arming the abaQulusi for future use as scouts. They were not under the command of Dinuzulu but of the British and they proved to be a very valuable addition to military operations.

Towards the end of 1900 the war had become a guerrilla insurrectionist conflict and the more regular British troops found it very difficult to pin down the Boer guerrillas. On 25 March 1901 the British declared martial law north of the Thukela River. Under the command of Colonel H. B. Bottomley and white officers, Zulu were armed and led on raids against Boers, primarily to take cattle, disarm Boers and bring the booty back to Zululand. The Zulu were promised ten per cent of any loot; the British were to take twenty-five per cent and the remainder would be reserved by Bottomley. Bottomley organized the construction of a fort barely a kilometre from uSuthu. It was to be used as a storage depot and armoury and from here guns and ammunition were to be supplied to the Zulu.

Dinuzulu's supporters were given upwards of 3,000 rifles. He was very careful in choosing only his most trusted indunas and warriors, which became known as the iNkomendala. By 4 April 1901 6,000 Zulu, under the command of Dinuzulu and Bottomley, mustered at uSuthu. A military expedition had been planned; the army would march north to Dlek Hill, forty kilometres from Nongoma. Here a number of Boers had settled with their cattle. The iNkomendala were in action between 4–9 April and succeeded in decisively defeating the Boers, taking thousands of cattle and hundreds of guns, together with several thousand rounds of ammunition which had been abandoned.

By 2 June 1901 the British considered that the Zulu had contributed enough to operations and the process of arming

Dinuzulu's men ceased. He was allowed to keep 3,000 armed men at uSuthu as a reserve.

On 8 March 1902 Dinuzulu was requested to send a force of 250 men into the Vryheid area to assist General Bruce Hamilton in operations against the Boers. The Zulu army, actually numbering around 1,000 men, arrived on 22 March 1902. They were supported by a similar number of abaQulusi, led by Sikhobobo Sibiya. In conjunction with the British force they defeated the Boers and took several hundred of their cattle.

The Boers were fast losing the war and they determined to exact retribution on the Zulu. On 23 April 1902 a Boer force destroyed many of the abaQulusi kraals, appropriated their cattle and took the women and children to Vryheid. The operation was complete by 1 May. Sikhobobo and the abaQulusi immediately went on the offensive and on 6 May a pitched battle resulted in the deaths of fifty-six Boers and fifty-two Zulu.

When the war ended in 1902 Dinuzulu was given 100 cattle for his assistance, but the British required the guns and ammunition which had been given to him to be returned. Effectively, he returned to being a local induna. Also in 1902, having set aside reserves for the Zulu, the territory was opened to European settlement.

On 22 November 1905 magistrates in Zululand were given instructions to call together the chiefs and explain a new tax which was to be imposed on 20 January 1906. Natal was in a desperate economic state and the new tax would be applied to every individual over the age of eighteen who was not already paying a hut tax. The payment of £1 was to be levied from January 1906 and would have to be paid by 31 May. Although there was huge discontent, Dinuzulu and his immediate followers paid the tax, but the first problem arose as early as 17 January. A farmer, Henry Smith, had taken his workers to Camperdown to pay the tax. When they returned that evening one of his servants passed him a note and as he was reading it the man stabbed Smith and killed him. In the trial the servant cited the poll tax as being the reason for killing Smith. Just five days later the magistrate at Mapumulo was threatened by a mob. The intervention of Ngobizembe (the local chief) saved the magistrate from certain death.

There were similar disturbances up and down the country. On 7 February the magistrate of Umgeni was also threatened and on the following day Sub-Inspector Hunt, at the head of fourteen Natal policemen, was sent to arrest the armed men who had threatened the magistrate. They managed to arrest one of the ring-leaders at his kraal, but suddenly the policemen were surrounded. Hunt and one of the troopers were killed and the others fled to Pietermaritzburg.

On 9 February Sir Henry McCallum, the Governor, proclaimed martial law. He mobilized 1,000 men and placed them under the command of Colonel Duncan McKenzie. His force consisted of Natal Carbineers, two squadrons of the Border Mounted Rifles, a squadron of the Natal Royal Regiment and elements of C Battery, Natal Field Artillery, in addition to various service and auxiliary troops. McKenzie headed straight for the site of the killing of the two policemen. Two men were arrested, court-martialled, found guilty and executed. McKenzie went on to arrest another twenty-four men, who he also court-martialled; half of these were sentenced to death. Sentence was carried out near Richmond on 2 April. A few days after the situation appeared to have stabilized and McKenzie's force broke up. Elsewhere, Lieutenant Colonel G. Leuchars had led a force to quell rioting and unrest along the north coast. His force was also demobilized at the end of March.

It seemed that any threat of an uprising, particularly with the connivance of the Zulu royal family, was unlikely. But there was an uprising in the offing, although it did not come from Dinuzulu.

Bambatha (correctly Bhambada) kaMancinza was a chieftain of the amaZondi. He was based in the Ngome region and had been born around 1861 and had assumed the role of chieftain in June 1890. As it was he had a fairly bad reputation already. He was allegedly already in debt, he had been implicated in a number of cattle thefts, had a poor relationship with neighbouring farmers and had even been involved in local fighting between rival factions.

Bambatha adamantly refused to pay the poll tax; the date set for him to pay was 22 February and the local magistrate was informed that if he went to collect the tax he would be killed. Instead the magistrate instructed Bambatha to appear before him in Greytown on 22 February. Bambatha did not appear on the due date and his indunas told the magistrate that he had a stomach ache. The magistrate decreed that Bambatha was henceforth deposed with effect from 23 February and that his uncle, Magwababa, was to act as regent until Bambatha's brother was of age.

On 9 March, Major W. J. Clark left at the head of 100 Natal Mounted Police and a squadron of the Umvoti Mounted Rifles, heading for the Mpanza Valley, to arrest Bambatha. Bambatha had already slipped away across the Thukela River in order to seek the assistance of Dinuzulu at uSuthu. He asked Dinuzulu to look after his wife and children then headed north to hide in the Nkandla forest.

Bambatha returned to Mpanza on 31 March and seized Magwababa, who he proposed to kill, but the killing was stopped by Cakijana, one of Dinuzulu's personal attendants, who was with Bambatha. On 4 April Colonel Leuchars dispatched Lieutenant Colonel G. Mansel, at the head of 173 Natal Mounted Police and the Umvoti Mounted Rifles, to scour the Mpanza area in search of Bambatha. Here Mansel received intelligence that Bambatha and his followers intended to ambush him near Keate's Drift. There was a brief skirmish which claimed four of the troopers. Significantly, the body of one of the troopers had been mutilated, to be used by Bambatha's witchdoctor to create a medicine which would make the rebels impervious to the white men's bullets.

On 8 April Leuchars surrounded and destroyed Bambatha's kraal, but he had already fled into Zululand, making his way to Simoyi's kraal at the mouth of the Mome gorge. This lay within the territory of the amaCube, led by their chieftain, Sigananda kaSokufa. Sigananda had been born in 1811 and was a firm uSuthu supporter. He had been inducted into Dingane's inKulutshane regiment back in 1830 and had been present when Piet Retief had been killed at Dingane's instruction. He had fought at the battle of Ndondakusuka in 1856 had been active during the Anglo-Zulu War of 1879 and had provided Cetshwayo with refuge and assistance after his defeat at oNdini in 1883. On 17 April the amaCube rebelled.

Three days earlier the Natal government had issued a proclamation that they would pay £500 for Bambatha, dead or alive.

Natal had asked for British regulars to be made available to put down the rebellion which they feared would spread across the country, but it was rejected and the Natal militia was mobilized, supported by units from Transvaal. Indeed Transvaal supplied 500 men under Lieutenant Colonel W. F. Baker, for the coming campaign. They were collectively known as the Transvaal Mounted Rifles, actually consisting of elements of the Imperial Light Horse, the South African Light Horse, the Johannesburg Mounted Rifles, the Scottish Horse and the Northern, Eastern and Western Mounted Rifles. The overall commander for what was to become known as the Nkandla Operations was Colonel Duncan McKenzie. He was a Natal farmer who had been a member of the Natal Carbineers and had fought in, among others, the Anglo-Boer War.

McKenzie had a number of units available to him. At Dundee the Transvaal Mounted Rifles were supported by Royston's Horse, twenty-five men of the Natal Field Artillery, a part company of the Durban Light Infantry and various support staff. The Natal Carbineers were based at Helpmekaar. The Zululand Mounted Rifles and the Northern Districts Mounted Rifles were based at Ntingwe. At Fort Yolland he could call on the support of the Natal Naval Corps, an additional section of the Natal Field Artillery, 200 Natal Police and ninety of the Nongqai (Zululand native police). At Eshowe there were two companies of the Durban Light Infantry and a further half company at Gingindlovu. In total, he had access to over 2,400 men. Interestingly, the Indian population of Natal provided a volunteer stretcher bearer company, amongst whom was Sergeant Major Mohandas K. Gandhi. Although McKenzie's force was not huge and the vast majority of the men were part-timers, they were almost exclusively armed with bolt action magazine rifles. They also had access to quick firing artillery and machine guns.

By the time McKenzie entered the field, his numbers had swelled to upwards of 3,700, including all levies which had attached themselves for support. The area in which he proposed to sweep was a heavily forested mountain region. It would not be easy to track down Bambatha's guerrillas. The Nkandla forest was an ideal place in which the rebels could operate. McKenzie intended to surround the area and make sweeps across until Bambatha was cornered.

On 2 May a detachment of the Natal Carbineers managed to kill four rebels in a skirmish and on 3 May the magistrate of Mhlabatini was murdered near the White Umfolozi River. This was a considerable distance from Nkandla and it is believed that the murder was perpetrated to convince the local tribesmen to join in the revolt. It is believed that the magistrate was shot by Cakijana himself.

The troops from Dundee left for Nkandla on 3 May. Colonel Mansel was already in operations in the Nkandla forest, at the head of a detachment of the Durban Light Infantry and the Natal Mounted Rifles. They were supported by some Nongqai, Natal Police and Natal Naval Corps. Also with them were 400 levies. They were making for Cetshwayo's grave where, they had been informed, the rebels were congregating.

On 5 May Mansel's force was working its way along the Bobe Ridge over the Nsuze River. The column came under fire from rebel snipers, resulting in just a single man being wounded. Mansel's advance guard, commanded by Lieutenant Blamey, with a troop of Natal Mounted Rifles and supported by the Nongqai, was suddenly attacked by around 200 rebels. There were several casualties inflicted on Blamey's command, but the Lieutenant himself was later awarded a Distinguished Conduct in the Field (he had been recommended for the Victoria Cross) for saving one of his troopers, who had been wounded and unhorsed. The rebels, the majority of whom were from Sigananda's tribe, were driven off with heavy casualties; at least fifty-five bodies were found in the immediate vicinity and it is believed that many more later died from their wounds.

The rebels headed back to Mome gorge to link up with Bambatha. He was assailed with accusations that his claim that the rebels would be immune to the white man's bullets was a lie. There was even talk that he should be turned over to the British. As it was Bambatha and his followers made for Macala Mountain, while Sigananda and his men hid in the Mome gorge. Mansel decided not to give pursuit and retired through the Nsuze Valley back to Fort Yolland.

By mid-May Bambatha had been joined by Mhlokazulu ka Sihayo (son of Sihayo). He remained at his camp at Macala. Colonel McKenzie, meanwhile, received intelligence that Sigananda and 1,000 of his tribesmen had moved back to the area around Cetshwayo's grave. McKenzie determined to manoeuvre three columns of troops and launch an assault on Sigananda on 16 May. McKenzie's force moved along the Nomangci Ridge, heading for the region where the Mome and Nsuze Rivers met. Colonel W.F. Barker, at the head of the Transvaal troops, moved from Ntingwe to the Nsuze River. Meanwhile Mansel's force left Yolland and headed up the Nsuze River. McKenzie also gave Leuchars instructions to leave the Middle Drift and attack Bambatha's warriors at Macala.

Both McKenzie and Barker arrived at their appointed jumping off points at 11.00 on 16 May. But as a result of Mansel's column arriving late, Sigananda and his men were able to slip deeper into the Mome gorge. During Barker's march to the gorge he had been attacked by some of Bambatha's rebels. Leuchars managed to drive Bambatha's men away from Macala and into the Qudeni forest. The only real success of this operation was that McKenzie had managed to capture the bulk of the rebels' cattle and goats.

McKenzie had established his base near Cetshwayo's grave and had resolved to sweep the gorge and force Sigananda to surrender. He deployed one of the Natal Field Artillery guns overlooking the Mome Valley and began to make preparations. Some time before 20 May a rebel messenger was told by McKenzie that he would give Sigananda until 11.00 on 20 May to surrender. But the appointed time came and went with no sign of Sigananda. McKenzie then extended the surrender date to 22 May. On 22 May Sigananda sent a message to McKenzie, telling him that he wanted to surrender in the Nkandla forest, agreeing to meet him at 11.00 on 24 May. McKenzie left Barker in command of a detachment at Cetshwayo's grave and at the head of a column, including Royston's Horse, the Northern Districts Mounted Rifles, the Zululand Mounted Rifles and two companies of the Durban Light Infantry, McKenzie headed towards Nkandla.

They reached their destination at 17.00 on 23 May. Again the appointed surrender time came and went. McKenzie then received a report that Bambatha was intending to move down from Qudeni to join up with Sigananda. McKenzie therefore began a night march towards Ensingabantu in order to encircle Bambatha. McKenzie's men arrived at this destination at 04.00. The area was shrouded in mist and when the mist lifted at 07.00, it was clear that Bambatha had slipped away; McKenzie then marched his troops back to Nkandla.

McKenzie now set up his base of operations at Nomangci, between the Mome gorge and Nkandla. On 29 May there was another major skirmish at the Tathe gorge, to the north of Mome. Hundreds of cattle were captured and forty rebels killed.

On 1 June two artillery pieces and two Pompom guns of the Natal Field Artillery began firing into the Mome gorge, concentrating on the area in which they believed the rebels were encamped. An hour after the guns opened fire, 100 Nongqai (under Inspector Fairlie), 400 Royston's Horse (under Colonel Royston), 150 Zululand Mounted Rifles (under Major Vanderplank), 140 Durban Light Infantry (under Major Molyneux), 100 Natal Police (under Sub-Inspector White) and 800 Native levies (under Lieutenant London) advanced down the gorge. It was 07.30. The net result of the operation was three rebel dead and twenty-four surrenders.

Sigananda could not be found, but the troops burned his eNhlweni kraal. The guns continued firing into the gorge until 19.00 the following day. On 3 June further sweeps were made through the surrounding forest area. Royston's Horse was ambushed at Manzipambana and it was only the timely arrival of reinforcements, led by Royston, which prevented Captain Clerk's men from being overrun. Nonetheless, five were killed and nine wounded. By the end of this phase of the operations 200 cattle had been captured and around 150 rebels killed. McKenzie, however, had not achieved what he had set out to do and that was to force the rebels into a major battle.

Meanwhile, Bambatha was trying to swing prominent Zulu behind his rebellion. He had already enlisted the support of Mangathi (son of Godide). Godide, it was later alleged, had slipped away to Nongoma, to visit Dinuzulu. The exact nature of their conversation still remains hotly disputed. According to one account, which would later damn Dinuzulu, he gave his tacit support to the rebellion, or at least Dinuzulu encouraged Mangathi to combine his forces with Bambatha and Mehlokazulu. There may have been a reason for this, as it had reached Dinuzulu's ears from Sigananda that white soldiers had desecrated Cetshwayo's gave. At least officially, Dinuzulu had made an offer of support to the British to help deal with the rebellion, but the truth is probably somewhere in the middle. Dinuzulu probably hoped that the rebellion would help convince the British that some of the grievances supported by the rebels needed to be addressed. Dinuzulu did know, however, that if he fully supported an armed insurrection then the cost in lives and his own power would undoubtedly be immeasurable.

On 9 June, McKenzie had received word from three members of the Zululand Mounted Rifles, Lieutenant Hedges, Sergeant Calvery and Sergeant Titlestad, who were all from prominent Zululand families. They had been trying to contact Sigananda. Sergeant Calvery had recognized one of the rebel prisoners and convinced him to accompany them to the Mome gorge and ask to speak to Mandisindaba, Sigananda's son, whom Calvery also knew. The meeting was arranged and Mandisindaba told Calvery that both he and his father truly wished to put an end to the conflict. During the same conversation Calvery discovered that Bambatha and Mehlokazulu were en route to the Mome gorge with a force of 1,000 warriors. They were due to arrive that very night.

McKenzie was immediately informed and he now realized that this was the opportunity for which he had been waiting. The informant had said that Bambatha had with him twenty amaviyo (companies) and therefore the total number of warriors could be as many as 3,000, as an amaviyo ranged in size from 50 to 150 men. Clearly, Bambatha's intention was to link up with Sigananda. McKenzie had to stop Bambatha from getting into the gorge, as once he was in there it would be almost impossible to force him out.

As Colonel McKenzie was not briefed on the new intelligence until 21.30 that night, he realized he would have to move fast. The first problem was to get a message through some twenty or more kilometres of rebel-held territory, to Barker, who was still at

Cetshwayo's grave. Three troopers made the perilous journey and reached Barker at 01.15 the following morning. The dispatch still exists and clearly outlines McKenzie's intentions:

> On receipt of this despatch, you will please move at once with all available men (leaving sufficient for the defence of your camp) to the mouth of the Mome Valley. I have information that an impi is coming from Qudeni to enter the Mome Valley between this and tomorrow morning. Please try to waylay this impi and prevent them from entering the Mome, and at daylight block the mouth of the Mome at once. It is anticipated that they will not enter the Mome till daylight. I have reliable information as to almost the exact spot Sigananda is in and I am moving down to surround him. He is supposed to be just below the Mome stronghold, a little lower down than where we burnt his kraal. I will cut off this position at daylight and drive down towards you, so please do all you can to prevent his escape, and cooperate with me generally.
>
> At daylight, please send the Zululand Police and Native levies up to Sigananda's kraal, which you burnt the day we attacked the stronghold, where they will join my forces. You must take your gun and Maxims in case you meet the impi, which is reported to be of strength. Look out for my signals.

The message was sent at 22.30 on 9 June 1906 from McKenzie's camp on the Nomangci.

Battle focus

Mome Gorge

10 June 1906

Bambatha was moving to the Mome gorge partly in response to a demand from Sigananda that he return and the misbelief that Barker was no longer at Cetshwayo's grave. This was based on intelligence that he and his wagons had gone back to Fort Yolland. In fact only the

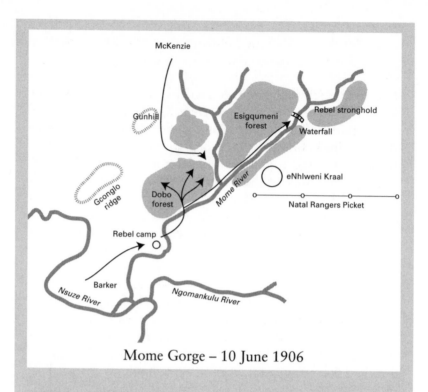

McKenzie

Gunhill

Esigqumeni
forest

Rebel stronghold

Waterfall

Gcongio
ridge

Dobo
forest

Mome River

eNhlweni Kraal

Natal Rangers Picket

Rebel camp

Barker

Nsuze River

Ngomankulu River

Mome Gorge – 10 June 1906

wagons had been sent out of the area. Bambatha's men
began moving towards the Mome gorge during the evening
of 9 June.

Barker, having received the message from McKenzie,
began moving his troops from their base camp (which was
five kilometres from Cetshwayo's grave) at around 02.00 on
10 June. With him were three squadrons of the Transvaal
Mounted Rifles, ninety Natal Police, two artillery pieces,
one Maxim gun and one Colt gun of the Natal Field
Artillery, around 100 Nongqai and Mfungelwa and Hatsi's
800 Native levies. Inspector Fairlie with the Nongqai and the
Native levies moved into position, overlooking a bend in
the Mome River. This was a narrow choke point and it was
Fairlie's responsibility to check any rebel movement
through the pass. Assuming he had not seen anything by
daylight, he was to make his way towards eNhlweni

(Sigananda's destroyed kraal) and link up with McKenzie. The rest of Barker's force continued along the Mome gorge until they saw a large number of campfires in a mealie field in a loop of the Mome River. It was obvious that the rebels were encamped here. Barker deployed two squadrons of the Transvaal Mounted Rifles on a ridge to the east, while his remaining squadron and fifty Natal Police occupied a ridge to the west of the entrance to the gorge. He retained some Natal Police as a reserve.

Mangathi had already joined Sigananda's encampment near the waterfall. But Bambatha and Mehlokazulu, along with the main rebel impi, had encamped at the mouth of the gorge, intending to join Sigananda the following morning.

At 03.00, Lieutenant Colonel J. Dick had left at the head of the Natal Rangers. Their role in the operation was to sweep around to the south and prepare a picket line to prevent the rebels from escaping when McKenzie's main force arrived from the north-east. Also at around 03.00 Lieutenant Colonel J. S. Wylie, commanding 140 men of the Durban Light Infantry, crossed the Nomangci Ridge and made for London Kop, which overlooked the Nsuze River. At 03.30 a squadron of Natal Carbineers, under Captain G. R. Richards, followed the same route taken by Wylie. His group was followed by Major Abraham, leading 100 Northern District Mounted Rifles, supported by Major Vanderplank at the head of 100 Zulu Mounted Rifles, two Pompom guns and an artillery piece of the Natal Field Artillery, a Maxim detachment and Royston's Horse.

Around 03.30 Bambatha was awoken by the news that the British advance had been spotted. The impi immediately prepared to move.

McKenzie had not anticipated that the battle would begin before daylight. But at 06.50 Captain H. McKay, of the Transvaal Mounted Rifles, who was only 200 metres from the rebel encampment, passed word to Lieutenant R. G. Forbes, commanding another squadron of the mounted troops, that the rebels were about to move. Forbes began opening fire with his Maxim gun. The opening shots acted as a signal and all of Barker's deployed men began firing into the rebel encampment. McKenzie quickly reacted to the firing; he was beginning to move towards the waterfall, where he believed Sigananda was encamped, but he recalled his men and sent them west, realizing that if the rebels were already engaged by Barker they would try to slip through the Dobo forest. Fairlie had already anticipated this and had sent twenty Nongqai and 400 of his Native levies to occupy the ground where the Dobo forest touched the Mome River. As McKenzie's men headed west and had nearly reached Gun Hill, he could see one of Barker's artillery pieces firing. He deployed his men on Gun Hill, leaving his artillery piece and Pompom guns to deploy, then wheeled his other troops around to cover the northern edge of Dobo forest. With the bulk of his troops in place, McKenzie deployed detachments of the Durban Light Infantry, Natal Carbineers and Northern Districts Mounted Rifles to the east of the forest to cover the last possible escape route. They arrived in the nick of time as Bambatha's warriors were already streaming through the forest.

By 08.00 McKenzie's artillery was firing at the stronghold, while Barker's artillery had moved up and was firing into the Dobo forest. Bambatha's men were trapped and McKenzie began to move his troops steadily through the Dobo forest. By the time all of his men were in position and had begun their careful search, it was around 14.00. At some point during this part of the operation Mehlokazulu was killed.

By 16.30 the rebels had been squeezed into a small section of the forest. A misinterpreted bugle signal, however, halted the sweep and around 100 rebels were able to escape. The skirmishing and hand-to-hand combat in the forest, added to the artillery fire, had accounted for nearly 600 rebels, including Mehlokazulu and four other key leaders.

Two or three men had been killed from McKenzie's force in addition to a number of wounded. There was still, however, no sign of Bambatha or Sigananda.

174

As far as McKenzie was concerned the operation had been a complete success, but he was still concerned that Bambatha and Sigananda had not been accounted for. Certainly the rebellion had been crushed, but the nagging concern that the two men were still at large meant that McKenzie and his men could not rest.

On 13 June one of the captured rebels identified himself as Bambatha's personal servant. He reported to McKenzie that Bambatha was dead; he had been killed just minutes after the shelling had begun in the Dobo forest. One of the Native levies had seen an unarmed rebel walking through the river. When the man reached the right bank the levy had stabbed him with an assegai, but he could not retract the blade. They had both fallen and a second levy had arrived to finish the man off. The rebel had grabbed the second man's assegai and the three had struggled. Suddenly a Nongqai had arrived and placed his rifle against the rebel's head and shot him with a dum-dum bullet. Sergeant Calverley headed a patrol to investigate and find the body. They did indeed find a rebel's corpse, but it was badly decomposed and almost unidentifiable. Calverley decapitated the corpse and put the head into his saddlebag, taking it back to McKenzie's camp. It appears that there was general consent that it was indeed Bambatha. The head was later returned to the Mome Gorge, where it was buried with the rest of the body on the right bank of the river.

Two alternative accounts, however, are worthy of mention. Firstly, a photograph was published in the Nongqai magazine in September 1925. It purported to depict Bambatha's shield, mounted upon which was a skull which was claimed to be that of the rebel leader. Alternatively, however, Bambatha's wife and her daughter disappeared shortly after the rebellion had been put down. It is said that they journeyed to Mozambique to be reunited with Bambatha, who had escaped the massacre at the gorge.

Calverley was again instrumental in securing Sigananda's surrender. He persuaded the chief's representative that unless he turned himself in to the authorities, McKenzie's troops would simply set the whole forest alight and let them burn. On 13 June 1906 Calverley brought in Sigananda to McKenzie's camp at Nomangci, where Lieutenant Colonel Wylie accepted his surrender in McKenzie's absence. The old chief was imprisoned at Nkandla on 16 June and tried on 21 June; he died the following day of natural causes.

The action at Mome Gorge did not, however, see the end of the rebellion. On 19 June there had been an uprising at Mapumulo, on the Thukela River. By this time the authorities were prepared to use any means to quell rebellion. Kraals were burned and cattle were confiscated. Any sign of resistance brought immediate retribution in the form of arrests, beatings and summary executions. It has been estimated that upwards of 4,000 rebels and rebel sympathizers had been killed by the beginning of September and a further 7,000 were in prison. Many of these men were used as virtual slave labour by Natal's public works department. There was considerable circumstantial evidence that Dinuzulu was implicated in the rebellion and there were many who were prepared to come forward and testify that he had been the driving force behind the revolt.

Dinuzulu was arrested on 9 December 1907 and he was taken to Greytown to stand trial for high treason. He was found not guilty of many of the charges levelled against him, but he could not deny that he had given support and shelter to some of Bambatha's followers and family. He was specifically found guilty of assisting Bambatha and Mangathi and some other 125 rebels, for which he was given four years. He was given a further year and a £100 fine for giving safe haven to Bambatha's wife and children. He was further stripped of his position as an induna. Dinuzulu was sent to Pietermaritzburg and then on to Newcastle, but when South Africa gained independence in 1910, Louis Botha, who had fought at the battle of Tshaneni as part of the Boers supporting Dinuzulu's army, allowed him to be released.

Dinuzulu was moved to a farm; he was in poor health and on 18 October 1913 he died as the result of various ailments, including Bright's disease. Dinuzulu would only ever return to Zululand for his burial. The last true king of the Zulu was dead and with him the military system, which had been wrought by Shaka less than 100 years earlier, died too.

Appendix One

The Zulu Regiments

Prior to the British attempt, shortly before the Anglo-Zulu War of 1879, it is difficult to be positive about the creation and activities of the Zulu regiments. Indeed, European writers prior to this period relied on Zulu oral recollections of the regiments. Clearly, this means that many of the dates are best guesses, based on memories dating back to the Shaka period, or that of Dingane. There is, therefore, confusion regarding the names attributed to the companies (izigaba), the amabutho (age groups) as well as the kraals (amakhanda) to which the amabutho were attached or associated. There is also additional confusion in as much as Shaka and Mpande both created an uMbonambi regiment and Dingane and Mpande had a uDlambedlu regiment.

Shaka's emBelebeleni or emBelebele was almost certainly a title used to describe a number of different Zulu amabutho. EmBelebeleni almost certainly refers to a royal household (ikhanda) rather than a regiment as such. Shaka inherited men from his father's army, for what it was worth, the oldest of which may have been the amaWombe (clash of arms). These men would have been born, in all probability, between 1775 and 1785. The amaWombe was formed as a regiment in about 1816. The emBelebeleni also included Zwide's amaPhela (the cock-roaches) which had been incorporated into the Zulu army after his defeat. Both these men and the AmaKwenkwe carried brownish-grey shields and were born between 1801 and 1807. Another element of the emBelebeleni is mentioned; the uMpondozobekwapi, who carried red cow hide shields, possibly older than the other men. All of the latter elements of the emBelebeleni were formed by Shaka as regiments or elements of the regiment between 1821 and 1827.

Shaka may have also inherited the isiklebhe (based as the ikhanda isikhebheni). This smaller ibutho had been formed by Senzangakhona in 1816; they carried grey shields and had probably been born during the period 1790 to 1795.

Shaka's uFasimba (distant blue haze), perhaps the best known, was formed around 1818 of men who had been born between 1795 and 1798. The regiment was to carry white shields.

Chronologically, Shaka formed the iziYendane in 1819; these men were Hlubi incorporated into Shaka's army as a result of his campaigning in the Drakenberg region. The iziYendane carried red shields. One of the most confusing of Shaka's formations was the isiPhezi (to stop). It may have either been otherwise known as the uMgumanqa (spoilers) or the iNtontela (fear). Be that as it may, the situation is further confused by the fact that another ibutho, the amaGoun, may have been incorporated into the uDlangubo, who in turn had been incorporated into the iNtontela. The original members of the isiPhezi were either born in the period 1789 to 1799, or may have been older. It is believed that the isiPhezi carried predominantly white shields with either red or black flecks or speckles.

The uZibolela (or uMbonambi) were men who had been born during the period 1801 to 1807. The regiment was formed over the period 1821 to 1827. uMbonambi means those who experience sorrow.

The uDlangezwa was created in 1823, from men who had been born in 1802 or thereabouts. The regiment carried predominantly black shields, but with numerous white spots. The regiment's name comes from dla (to destroy an enemy) and ngezwa (meaning to hear). Chronologically, the next regiment to be created was the uHlotane, possibly in 1825, but little is known about the unit.

The izimPohlo was not a regiment, but a brigade (either brigaded by Shaka or later by Dingane). In any case, all the regiments associated with the izimPohlo were stationed by Dingane at Mgungundlova ikhanda. It is believed that the regiments consisted of men born between 1801 and 1807 and that the formations were created by Shaka between 1821 and 1826. Some six regiments are associated with the izimPohlo brigade but more is known about some of the regiments than others. The uGibabanye (the ousters), who may have also been known as the uPhoko (millet) were believed to have carried black shields with some with patches on the sides of the shields. Incorporated within the uPhoko or uGibabanye were the uMpotu (who carried grey-brown shields) and the uMnyama (who had black shields). Both the uFojisa and the Ngqobolondo were also brigaded into the izimPohlo; they both had predominantly black shields, the former with white patches and the latter with white speckles. The uShoyisa, which were believed to be part of the uFojisa carried red shields with white markings. The izimPohlo was completed with the much lesser known uMfolozi and the uDubinhlangu.

Shaka's uBhenkenya is closely associated with the iNgcobinga (or uJubingqwanga). The uBhenkenya (or iNdabankhulu), known as the 'big affair' was formed around 1827 and carried black shields with white markings. At some point, it does appear that the uBhenkenya were incorporated into the iNgcobinga. The iNgcobinga was formed in 1828, primarily from men who were born in 1808. The regiment's alternative name, uJubingqwanga, may mean or refer to the word 'locust'. The regiment was renamed by Dingane as the iziNyosi (bees) and they probably carried grey shields with white speckles.

Dingane's regiments are, at first, confused by the concepts of the Hlomenlini mhlope and the Hlomendlini mayama (respectively meaning white troops and black troops armed at home). This undoubtedly refers to Dingane's amakhanda and should not be confused with the names of the regiments themselves.

As we have seen, the iziNyosi had been formed from Shaka's own iNgcobinga. Dingane's first true regiment was created in 1820 from men who had been born around 1809; the uDlambedlu (those who worry at a thing and eat it up). It is not known what colours were favoured by the regiment on its shield. The imiKhulutshane (stumbling blocks) were created around 1833 from men born in 1813. Shortly after the imVokwe (subjugators) were formed around 1835 from men born in the period around

179

1815. The iHlaba (the stabbers) were formed quite probably in 1837, the men having been born twenty or so years prior to this date. They carried predominantly black shields with some white spots. The regiment may have been otherwise known as the iziNgulutshane or the izinDabakadengizbona. The final two regiments of Dingane's reign were the uKhokothi (named after a snake) and the iNsewane (sharp youths). The former were created in 1836 to 1838 and the latter right at the very end of Dingane's rule (1838 to 1840). The men would have been born between 1817 and 1820.

Dingane's regiments were, as we will see, merged with the newly created regiments of Mpande. Mpande's first new regiment, the iNdabakawombe (iNdaba meaning ambush and wombe meaning clash of arms) was created in 1841 (men born in 1821). It was merged with Dingane's uKhokothi (formed 1837 to 1838). The regiment itself carried white shields and the ceremonial headgear included ostrich feathers and crane feathers. It may be possible that the regiment additionally wore lourie and eagle feathers.

Mpande's second regiment, the uDlambedlu, was created in 1843 and was merged with Dingane's regiment, the iNsewane, of men born in 1823. In later years the iNgwege (hooked stick) and the uMdlenevu (burnt sides) were merged. It is probable that the uDlambedlu carried predominantly white shields with black or red speckles.

Dingane's original uDlambedlu is most closely associated with Mpande's izinGulube. The latter regiment may well have been formed to act as a feeder unit for the older regiment. The izinGulube (sometimes known as the iNkone – meaning black and white pigs) was created in 1845 from men born twenty years earlier.

Mpande created the Isangqu (or amaShishi) in 1848 (men born around 1828). Initially they were issued with black shields, but by the British invasion of 1879 they had white shields. The regiment's name, Isangqu, means the hunters.

It is believed that the uThulwana, created in 1850, were named after the BaSotho chieftain Thulane. It contained a group called the iNhlambamasoka (amongst whom were Cetshwayo and other princes). The regiment was also called the amaBoza and the men

180

would have been born around 1830. It was later merged with the iNkonkoni (created 1852) and the iNdlondlo (created 1853). Initially, the uThulwana carried black shields with some white spots to the bottom of the shield, but by 1879 the shields were white with some red patterning.

The men born around 1835 were mustered into the uDlokwe or uDloko regiment in 1855. To begin with the regiment had red shields, but by the 1879 war the shields had acquired white patches or were wholly white.

Incorporated within the uDududu (created 1857) were the iMbube (formed in the same year from men born around 1837). The regiment carried black shields with some white markings towards the bottom of the shield. The iQwa was formed by Mpande in 1860 from men born twenty years before; it may have operated separately for some time but was, in all probability, merged into the uDududu. The iNsukamngeni were, in turn, incorporated into the iQwa, being of the same age group. The iQwa are described as having either black and white or red and white shields. It is probable that the black and white option is more viable on account of the fact that the iNsukamngeni had black shields with white markings on the bottom of the shield. Some accounts suggest that the uMxapho were part of the uDududu regiment, but they are probably just closely related (uphalane). The regiment was formed around 1860 of twenty-year old men. Umxapho means 'the mongrels', but later the regiment would be referred to as the iMpunga (the grey headed ones that do not die). This new name would have to wait until after the battle of Nyezane on 22 January 1879. It is believed that the uMxapho carried black shields with some white spots.

In 1862 the men born in 1842 were drafted into the uMbonambi regiment; the regiment's title meaning those who experience sorrow. The uMbonambi was also known as the iNkonyane-bomvu (red calf). The regiment was in the vanguard of the hand-to-hand fighting at Isandlwana. They carried either black shields or black shields with some white spots or speckles.

The uNokhenke consisted of the men born in 1845 and was raised in 1865. uNokhenke may mean 'the skirmishers'. The regiment carried either pure black shields or black shields with some white spots. Two years later the iNdluyengwe was created. Although it would be merged into Cetshwayo's uThulwana, iNdluyengwe (leopard's red markings) unsurprisingly wore leopard-skin headbands and carried black shields with white markings at the bottom.

The uKhandempemun (head with black and white markings) is better known as the uMcijo (red needle with two points). The regiment was created in 1868 and was made up of twenty-year old warriors. It had two main groupings within the regiment which were the uMtulisazwe (to make peace) and the iNgqakamatshe (stone catchers). It seems that the regiment had a wide variety of shields, but mainly black or dark brown with some white spots or patches on one side, some with black shields and a single white spot or wholly white shields.

In 1872 the iNgobamakhosi (the humblers of kings) were formed. The men had been born in 1853. The vast majority of the shields were dark brown (perhaps mottled) with irregular white patches. Other descriptions of their shields include black and red with or without spots.

Towards the end of the 1840s Mpande may have begun to form another regiment, the amaPhela, but it appears that the men originally assigned for this regiment were ultimately deployed as members of the iNdabakawombe and the uDlambedlu.

Cetshwayo's only contribution to the Zulu army was the uVe (fly catchers). It was also known as the oLandandlovu (elephant fetchers). The regiment was created between 1875 and 1878 from men who had been born between 1855 and 1858. The regiment may have carried a mixture of black and brown shields, perhaps some which were red with white spots. In any case, the uVe was merged with the iNgobamakhosi on the eve of the war in 1879.

Appendix Two

Timeline

Year	Event
1787	Shaka is born
1802	Shaka and Nandi settle within the Mthethwa land
1816	Senzangakhona dies Shaka becomes Zulu chieftain
1818–19	Campaigns against Zwide's Ndwandwe
1820–24	Shaka consolidates his conquests
1824	Zulu raid the amaMpondo (southern Natal) Farewell and Fynn visit kwaBulawayo Attempt on Shaka's life
1826	Campaign against the Ndwandwe
1827	Somerset destroys the Ngwane at the Battle of Mbolompo Campaign against the Khumalo Cetshwayo born Shaka's diplomatic mission to the Cape
1828	Zulu diplomatic mission to the Cape Colony (23 September) Shaka assassinated Second campaign against the amaMpondo Campaign against Soshangane

Year	Event
1828 *(cont.)*	Mbulazi born Dingane accedes to the throne
1829	Dingane builds umGungundlovu
1830	Dingane's diplomatic mission to Natal
1832	Campaign against Mzilikazi
1833	Zulu troops burn kraals around Delagoa Bay
1835	Great Trek begins
1836	Campaign against the Swazi
1837	Boers attack Mzilikazi (6 February) Piet Retief and his followers killed at umGungundlovu Dingane's second campaign against Mzilikazi
1838	(17 February) Zulu attacks on Boers in the Drakensberg (10 April) Battle of eThaleni (17 April) Battle of the Thukela (13 August) Renewed Zulu attacks on the Drakensberg (16 December) Battle of Blood River
1839	Mpande allies with the Boers against Dingane
1840	Battle of amaQongo (21 January) Pretorius and his commando enter Zululand (10 February) Mpande proclaimed king
1842	(1 April) Smith's force leaves amaMpondoland (4 May) Smith enters Durban (23 May) Smith beaten off in attack on Congella by the Boers (Mid-June) Boer siege raised (31 August) Natal accepts British rule (5 October) British sign treaty with Mpande ceding St Lucia Bay to the British
1845	Natal becomes a British colony

Year	Event
1848	Langalibalele's amaHlubi driven into Natal (3 February) British annex the territory between the Orange and Vaal Rivers
1849	James Rorke builds Rorke's Drift on the Buffalo River
1852	Zulu raid the Swazi British and Boers sign the Sands River Convention, recognizing Boer claims north of the Vaal
1856	Zulu civil war breaks out (2 December) Battle of Ndondakusuka Mbulazi enters Zululand
1863	Smallpox sweeps Natal
1864	Mtonga flees to Natal
1872	Mpande dies
1872–75	Lung sickness decimates the Zulu cattle
1873	(1 September) Cetshwayo accedes to the throne and builds oNdini
1874	(12 March) Natal Mounted Police formed
1876	(September) Zulu attack Tonga kraal
1877	(12 April) British annex Transvaal The uThulwana and the iNgobamakosi clash at oNdini
1878	(4 March) Frederic Augustus Thesiger appointed Commander of British Troops in South Africa (7 March) Boundary Commission convenes at Rorke's Drift (29 July) Two of Sihayo's wives cross into Natal with their lovers (11 December) Findings of the Boundary Commission delivered. Shepstone reads intention to the Zulu representatives

Year	Event
1879	(11 January) Frere publishes notification of British intention to invade Zululand
	(12 January) British attack Sihayo's kraal
	(17 January7) Durnford's column moves to Rorke's Drift
	(17 January) Centre column establishes camp at Isandlwana
	(20 January) Chelmsford arrives at Isandlwana
	(20 January) Wood reaches the White Umfolozi
	(21 January) British mounted troops scout surrounding area toward oNdini
	(22 January) Chelmsford leaves to support Dartnell, leaving Pulleine in command at Isandlwana
	(22 January) Battle of Isandlwana
	(22 January) Battle of Nyezane
	(22–23 January) Battle of Rorke's Drift
	(23 January) Pearson begins to establish camp at Eshowe
	(12 March) Battle of Ntombe River
	(28 March) Battle of Hlobane
	(29 March) Battle of Khambula
	(2 April) Battle of Gingindlovu
	(2 June) Prince Imperial killed
	(4 July) Battle of oNdini
1883	(10 January) Cetshwayo returns to Zululand
	(30 March) Battle of Msebe
	(May – June) Cetshwayo musters his warriors at oNdini
	(20 July) Zibhebhu musters his army at ekuVukeni and marches for the Mahlabathini plain
	(21 July) Second Battle of oNdini – Cetshwayo captured and sent into exile
1884	(8 February) Cetshwayo dies
	(21 May) Dinuzulu proclaimed king
	(3 June) Dinuzulu's army arrives at Bangonome
	(5 June) Battle of eTshaneni

Year	Event
1887	(9 May) Zululand becomes a British colony
1888	Zulu uprising – Dinuzulu sent into exile Hut tax imposed in Zululand
1893	(23 June) Shepstone dies
1895	Locust plague in Zululand (5 August) Dunn dies
1897	Tongoland annexed to Zululand (13 December) Zululand becomes part of Natal
1902–4	Zululand Lands Delimitation Commission sets reserves and land available to white farmers
1902	Zulu support British during the Boer War
1905	(August) Poll tax imposed in Zululand
1906	(February) Violence in Richmond, Natal (ringleaders shot on 2 April) (4 April) Bambatha ambushes police Zulu rebellion: (10 June) Battle of Mome Gorge (23 July) Sigananda dies (September) Rebellion crushed
1913	(October) Dinuzulu dies
1916	Solomon (Maphumuzana) becomes king
1933	Solomon dies
1945	Cyrpian Bhekezulu becomes king

Bibliography

Becker, Peter, *Dingane: King of the Zulu 1828–1840.* Thomas Y. Crowell Co., 1964

Becker, Peter, *Hill of Destiny: The Life and Times of Moshesh, the Founder of the Basotho,* Longman, 1969

Becker, Peter, *Rule of Fear: the Life and Times of Dingane, King of the Zulu,* Penguin Books, 1979

Bleeker, Sonia, *The Zulu of South Africa: Cattlemen, Farmers, and Warriors,* William Morrow & Co., 1970

Berglund, Axel-Ivar, *Zulu Thought-patterns and Symbolism,* C. Hurst & Co., 1989

Binns, C.T. *Dinuzulu; the Death of the House of Shaka,* London, Longmans, 1968

Bulpin, T.V., *Shaka's Country – A Book of Zululand,* Cape Town, Howard Timmins, 1952

Champion, George, *Journal of the Rev. George Champion, American missionary in Zululand 1835–9,.* Edited and annotated by Alan R. Booth, Cape Town, C. Struik (Pty.) Ltd., 1967

Coupland, Sir Reginald, *Zulu Battle Piece,* London, Tom Donovan, 1991

Dodds, Glen Lyndon, *The Zulus and Matabele Warrior Nations,* London, Arms & Armour Press, 1998

Du Buisson, Louis, *The White Man Cometh,* Johannesburg, Jonathan Ball Publishers, 1987

Du Toit, Brian M., *Content and Context of Zulu Folk-Narratives,* University Press of Florida, 1989

188

Edgerton, Robert B., *Like Lions They Fought: The Zulu War and the Last Black Empire in South Africa*, Ballantine Books, 1998 (Reprint)

Forsyth, D. R. & Trevor J. Davies (Editor), *Zulu Rebellion, 1906*, Roberts Medals Publications, 1990

Gray, Stephen, *The Assassination of Shaka*, McGraw Hill Book Company, Johannesburg, 1974

Gump, James Oliver, *The Formation of the Zulu Kingdom in South Africa, 1750–1840*, Edwin Mellen Press, 1991

Guy, Jeff, *The Destruction of the Zulu Kingdom*, University of Natal Press, 1996

Haggard, H.R., *Cetewayo and His White Neighbours; or Recent Events in Zululand*, Natal and the Transvaal, 1891, 4th edn

Hamilton, Carolyn, *Terrific Majesty. The Powers of Shaka Zulu and the Limits of Historical Invention*, Cape Town, David Philip, 1998

Knight, Ian J., *Warrior Chiefs of Southern Africa: Shaka of the Zulu, Moshoeshoe of the BaSotho, Mzilikazi of the Matabele, Maqoma of the Xhosa*, Firebird Books, 1994
Great Zulu Battles 1838–1906, Cassell, 1998
The Anatomy of the Zulu Army: From Shaka to Cetshwayo 1818–1879, Wrens Park Publishing, 1999
The National Army Museum Book of the Zulu Wars, Sidgwick and Jackson, 2003

Laband, John, *Rope of Sand*, Jonathan Ball Publishing, 1995
Rise and fall of the Zulu Nation, London, Arms & Armour Press, 1997
The Atlas of the Later Zulu Wars 1883–1888, University of Natal Press, 2002

Lock, Ron, *Blood on the Painted Mountain: Zulu Victory and Defeat, Hlobane and Kambula, 1879*, Greenhill Books, 1995

Lock, Ron and Peter Quantrill, *Zulu Victory: The Epic of Isandlwana and the Cover up*, Greenhill Books, 2002

Mann, Kenny, *Monomotapa, Zulu, Basuto: Southern Africa: African Kingdoms of the Past*, Dillon, 1996

Morris, Donald R., *The Washing of the Spears: The Rise & Fall of the Zulu Nation*, New York, Simon & Schuster Trade Paperbacks, 1986

Mulikita, F.M., *Shaka Zulu*, Lusaka, Longmans of Zambia, 1967

Rattray, David and Adrian Greaves, *David Rattray's Guide to the Zulu War*, Pen & Sword Books/Leo Cooper, 2003

Ritter E. A., *Shaka Zulu : The Rise of the Zulu Empire,* London, Longmans, 1955

Roberts, Brian, *The Zulu Kings: A Major Reassessment of Zulu History,* New York, Charles Scribner's Sons, 1974

Seed, Jenny, *The Voice of the Great Elephant,* New York, Pantheon, 1968 (Fiction)
Vengeance of the Zulu King, New York, Pantheon, 1970

Selby, John, *Shaka's Heirs,* George Allen & Unwin, 1971

Smail, J.L., *From the Land of the Zulu Kings,* Durban, 1979

Stuart, James, *The Diary of Henry Francis Fynn,* Compiled from original sources, Pietermaritzburg, Shuter & Shooter, 1950

Stuart, P.A., *An African Attila: Tales of the Zulu Reign of Terror,* Shuter & Shooter, Pietermaritzburg, 1938

Taylor, Stephen, *Shaka's Children : A History of the Zulu People,* Borgo Press, 1996

Tingay, Paul and Jill Johnson, *Transvaal Epic,* Natal, Khenty Press, 1978

Webb, Colin de B. & John B. Wright (Editors), *The James Stuart Archive of Recorded Oral Evidence Relating to the History of the Zulu and Neighbouring Peoples* Volumes 1–4, University of Natal Press, 1996

Index

196